The idea for this book started around fifteen years ago when I used to tell folks about my time with the band. 'Write a book' they would say. And here it is! I have had a great time delving through my memories and getting them into some sort of order. I have done it all on a normal desktop publishing package, laptop and mobile phone, and have nearly reached the edges of sanity when organising the page layout and pictures. Please excuse errors in dates and chronology, and also possible typos! The old grey matter is not what it was and the information all comes from memory – no notes.

Authors often dedicate books to special people so I will join the throng.

This is for Ben, Lucy, Poppy and Emmie with love from Grandad

The author at work.

Phil Rylance was born in Crewe, lived between the Manchester and Liverpool railway lines, passed the Chester line every day and went to school on the Derby line. His family has a total of one thousand years of railway employment since the 1830s. His generation was the first one not to be railway employees. He became a guitar player!

He now lives in Derbyshire.

Foreword

Early February 1962

The warehouse was just off Dale Street. It was small, dirty, smelly and thus was perfect for a club - The Iron Door. The stairs to the dressing room were narrow and steep and I half fell into the small room at the top.

'Y' alright,' said one of the three other occupants of the room.

'Fine thanks,' I said as I plonked the drum and guitar cases on the floor with a grin.

I surveyed the three guys who were sitting in a row on a small table; black clothes, medium size, leather flying boots for one of them and all three with hair long enough to get me thrown out of school on the following day.

'Want some coke?' asked the one on the end. 'You the other group? Where you from?'

'Thanks,' I said taking a swig. 'Crewe.'

'Whoa – Crewe - real foreigners,' laughed the one in the middle.

'I'm George,' said the one with the Coke bottle. 'This is John and Paul.'

After we'd done our first session I went down to watch the three guys play. Their drummer, a good-looking lad called Pete, joined them on the tiny stage and they went into Long Tall Sally. The hairs on the back of my neck leapt a mile as the electric atmosphere in the place ran wild. I had never in my eighteen years heard anything so full of life and enthusiasm. All the rules were broken; no rhythm guitar, they both played a sort of double lead, no handsome lead singer, no echo chamber for the voice and equipment that was old and knackered. But wow!

At the end of the night we picked up our twelve pounds and they got their twenty.

'See you in two weeks lads,' called John as we piled into our Morris Commercial ex Post Office van and headed off towards the tunnel, the Chester by-pass and home.

Chapter One

Early Days – The Elvis Inside

The musical Rylances outside the Ashbank Hotel 1955

It was all Peter Larcombe's fault. Not that he knows it, just like he doesn't know that he's on the first page of this book. It was the autumn of 1957 and Pete had advertised his guitar in the Crewe Chronicle for the princely sum of three pounds. Now three pounds in 1957 was a lot of money, especially if your dad was in the Machine Shop of British Railways as a fitter earning sixteen pounds a week.

I had taken a Thursday off school with a rumbling chest (everyone in Crewe had a rumbling chest from the steam trains and the factory chimneys) and there I was flicking through the paper when the musical instruments column soon made me forget the bronchials and cast my mind over to the hip swivelling, lip curling cowboy who'd been on at the Odeon cinema the previous week. If only I could get a guitar I told myself I could get up on stage and be a star.

To this day I don't know how I persuaded my mother to take me on the bus to look at the guitar but once I saw it I was hooked. It was about three-quarter size and had violin type machine heads to tune the strings. I reckon it was a Crewe works pattern-shop job, but that didn't matter. It was a guitar. I floated home on the Richmond Road bus complete with my new prize and immediately dashed upstairs to the bedroom I shared with my brother David to rehearse my hip swivels.

At this time I was fourteen and had been at St Joseph's High School in Stoke for three years. This was the nearest Catholic Grammar school to Crewe, so if you passed your eleven plus you had to trog twenty two miles every day courtesy of The Crosville Bus Company, British Railways and Potteries Motor Traction (to this day nobody believes me when I tell them that I went to school with PMT!).

I was proud of the fact that I played stand-off for the rugby team. I captained the under fourteens and eventually in the fifth form made the school first team. My scrum half was a guy called John Ridge who also was a guitar player and owned a Rolliford acoustic/electric which had a lovely sound. Each Saturday between the end of school and the beginning of the match we would borrow the school film projector, pick the lock to the school music room and plug in Rigger's guitar. An amazing three watts of unadulterated manic power leapt from the five inch speaker and we were off in a world of our own with about a dozen Catholic rugby players gyrating to the sounds of Bee Bop-a-Lula and Twenty Flight Rock. This all came to a sad end when old Sam Skaer, the music teacher, found out what his beloved music room was being used for.

'Jazz wops. That's what you are. Hooligans the lot of you.'

'No sir. Rock and roll.'

'Don't disagree with me boy. It's jazz, off beat, accent on the second and fourth of every bar.'

This was news to both Rigger and me so we decided to find out what a bar was.

However, back to the fourteen year old hip swiveller.

I tuned the guitar to a straight E chord and within a day could play Cumberland Gap and Freight Train. I was the original play-in-a-day wonder, but the hair looked good and the shirt collar turned up looked cool and mean! Little did I realise that the guitar had a completely different tuning and used to wonder why my efforts sounded different from Bert Weedon or Chet Atkins. Believe it or not I played with this tuning for about six months with Brother Dave on piano attempting to teach me the delights of traditional New Orleans Jazz as turned out by Chris Barber and Ken Collyer on the good old BBC Light Programme's Saturday Club with Brian Matthew. But Chris and Ken didn't have hips that swivelled or collars that turned up, but more importantly they were surrounded by bearded young men with pint pots, rather than young, pretty girls in hooped petticoat skirts.

After months of bashing and having finger ends that looked like tram tracks, the three hours a day paid dividends and I began to sound almost reasonable. I reckon I did the best Frankie Laine in Richmond Road, which wasn't difficult when you were the only guitar player and singer in Richmond Road. Eventually I found a book and realised my tuning errors. Within days I was back to square one with even deeper tram tracks on my left hand fingers. Would I ever be a star? Course I would. Just keep on trying.

At this time, I reckon it is well worth a look at the reasons behind the huge change in popular music and the bands and groups that played it. I think it all started with a concert at the Royal Festival Hall by Chris Barber's Jazz Band. The date-January 9th 1955. Barber's interval break came and about half his band disappeared for a pint, leaving Barber himself, bassist Jim Bray and his unknown banjo player whose name was Lonnie Donegan. Donegan changed banjo for guitar and went into an old American country folk song called Rock Island Line. This was Skiffle, a new music medium for British audiences, and the crowd went wild for the music and for Donegan. Why? I hear you ask. The simple answer is, it was music that everybody could play. There were no clever chord progressions like Cole Porter, no booming brass section like

8

Count Basie or Ted Heath and no full backing singers like The Platters. All you needed was a guitar, a tea chest bass of some sort and something to bash out a rhythm. Skiffle groups like The Vipers, Bob Cort, Chas McDevitt, Les Hobeaux and others sprang up all over the country and not long after, the electric guitar followed with people like Denny Wright and Big Jim Sullivan in UK. Kids bought guitars and drums and were eager to play the latest stuff they could hear on the radio.

At the same time a huge change in pop music styles came from the USA. Frank Sinatra, Frankie Laine and Johnny Ray were suddenly old hat and the world welcomed a brand new breed of tall, often gangly young men with guitars and more importantly, songs you could copy. I think the biggest influence of all was Buddy Holly. Many others will say Elvis, or Bill Haley, but local groups didn't have saxophones, and Elvis, with all his backing, was often not easy to copy at that time with limited group equipment. If you listen to the early Buddy Holly releases you can hear simple guitar chords, simple words and a very simple way of recording. 'Ooh Oopeydo, I love you'. This was heaven to young guys all over the UK and like me I reckon there were hundreds of would - be stars glued to Dansette record players or Radio Luxembourg with pen and paper at the ready to write down words and work out chords for that night's performance at the local village hall! Groups sprang up in every city, town and village throughout the land, all of them eager to knock out the latest version of Rave On or Peggy Sue, but where would they play?

In those days of the late fifties most towns had at least one or two fourteen piece dance bands playing regularly for promoters at the local hall. Crewe had two excellent bands playing regular gigs, both local and further afield. The Ralph Cowdell Orchestra and The Eric Latham Orchestra had many very good musicians who laid down great tunes for the dance craze of the late fifties. But things were soon to change. All of a sudden promoters realised that a four piece local group with electric amplifiers were just as loud as a fourteen piece band and also that they played more modern stuff that the new audiences loved. But to cap it all, a four piece in those days played for about ten or twelve pounds per night whereas the big bands needed about twenty five at least. Game, set and match to the groups! It was this great period of change that I joined as a fourteen year old with huge ambitions, hair growing longer and a ready smile. Thanks to the good old US of A, I was all set for stardom.

First ever publicity photo 1959

Chapter Two

The Journey Begins

At this time I met a young lad some two years younger than me who was to influence my world like no one else had done before. This was Keith Haines, otherwise known as Ted or Clank (don't ask 'cos I don't know). Ted was thirteen when we met and had a natural aptitude for the guitar. He could actually play solos like on real records in the Hit Parade. 'Twenty Flight Rock' and 'Mean Woman Blues' never sounded the same again. Ted would put in a loud, fuzzy, buzzing solo on a guitar that his brother Clive had made from a cut-down Spanish fingerboard, a plywood square and an old magnetic microphone pick up. Laugh you not! This was real Rock'n'Roll in capital letters. It was freedom and fresh air as never experienced before. Gone was the dirt, grime, soot and slog that was Crewe in the late fifties. We were transported to Nashville, L.A., Hollywood, anywhere! It is amazing what you can do when you are fifteen and have wide-open eyes and a fantastic will to fly.

Eventually I joined Ted's group. Now groups in those days were not like the modern televised, multi-coloured, expensively dressed young icons of today. We all wore white shirts with sleeves rolled up so that you could see what you were playing. Believe it or not there were very few pairs of jeans being worn in 1959, so dark trousers were the order of the day. However it was the equipment that was amazing. Every group of performers had a mate who knew about 'electricity and things', and who could build cabinets for speakers from old doors and packing crates etc. You went to gigs with homemade gear looking like crystal set technology and old Grundig tape recorder microphones. If you were extremely wealthy you might have a Watkins Dominator which boasted twenty watts of unadulterated power and twin eight-inch speakers, all decked out in a blue and white cabinet; eat your heart out Pete Townsend!

We started playing at Wistaston Memorial Hall dances on a Saturday in the interval between sessions from Jack Constadine and his record playing system. Jack was about fifty at the time and had large PA systems which he hired out to local agricultural shows and village fetes. He also had a record player that he linked to his amp and speakers and this became Crewe's first ever Disco!

Interspersed with Barn Dances and Gay Gordons, Jack would play the latest offerings from Elvis, Doris Day and British stars like Frankie Vaughan and Tommy Steele. We would come on at about half past eight and do a mixture of Lonnie Donegan Skiffle, Brenda Lee rock and roll and Jerry Lee Lewis country rock. We had a great piano man in Dave Jones whose dad was head of PE at the grammar school. Jonah went on to play bass with Lonnie Donegan for many years and eventually became Steve Jones, TV presenter of some long forgotten quiz show.

As we used to start our session a strange phenomenon occurred. All the girls and some of the boys would stop dancing and crowd round the front of the hall where we had set up. We soon realised that it was all very well being a star but not very comfortable to be stared at with every move and amateurish note being scrutinised to see how you measured up to the TV wonders. Mistakes were many and words were made up but at last we had started on the road to wherever it was that we were hopefully going. I think we were called The Rebels but it was fifty nine years ago at the time of writing and the old memory is not as crisp and clear as it once was.

After some time Ted and I decided that we wanted to progress beyond the Memorial Hall and formed our own group called The Echoes. We had business cards printed with both our names on and advertised as a rhythm group for dances, weddings and private functions. We co-opted Malc Steele, a young apprentice from the railway works, Bob Sant from Willaston, Skiff Becket from Lime Tree Estate as singer and Al Betts as drummer. Al had been in the navy and was a veteran aged about twenty, which seemed amazingly old to the rest of us who were about sixteen. We were contacted by the Co-op Youth Club to do a Friday night in their room above the café in, believe it or not, Co-op Street. We got ourselves practised up and went to the gig on the bus! I still cry with laughter when I look back and think of five skinny youths with lots of home-made equipment trying to look cool on a service bus bound for Market Street and the gig. I can also remember the fee of thirty shillings that we dutifully split at the end of the night. Six shillings was more than I had ever had in my life. As far as I can remember every gig by The Echoes was courtesy of the Crosville Bus Company, with Ted still being able to travel half-fare because of his age!

One memorable gig took place in the summer of 1961. We had been booked for Willaston Working Men's Club which is on the Nantwich Road from Crewe. We arrived and started to set up to find, as was common in those days, no suitable electric plug in socket for our stuff. We are talking here of the large round pin 15 amp sockets which were still common in a lot of places. We only had the smaller 5 amp round pin which of course was no good at all. Ingenuity took over and we decided to use the light socket from above the stage to plug in. Out came the bulb and in went our mains lead with a light attachment fitted. Obviously there was no earth connection so we simply left the earth wire hanging outside the attachment and wired the live and neutral. I can hear you now saying oh dear, oh dear, oh dear... and such was the case. We started playing and I decided that my voice was not being picked up well enough. I was playing my old Martin Colletti with a pick-up screwed on to the bottom of the neck. I started to lift the old heavy metal mike stand and put it between me and the guitar through the strap so that I could get really close. As I lifted it the stand touched the strings of the guitar.

The next thing I remember was being flung across the stage still clutching the stand and guitar unable to let go of either. I had the most agonising whirring sound in my ears and was pinned half way up the wall. I am still here today thanks to the quick thinking of Ted who whipped out the jack plug from my amp. I slumped to the floor amongst screams from the crowd and panic from everyone else. I had told everyone I wanted to make the girls scream but I didn't mean like this! 999 was dialled and the ambulance arrived very soon afterwards. I was carted off to Crewe Memorial Hospital and admitted. The doctor was very kind and stated that he did not know how I could possibly have survived! 'You should not be here, alive at this moment,' were his very words. Anyway all I had at that time was a burn on my middle finger, left hand where I was holding the stand. My Dad was working late at the time and had heard on the jungle telegraph that some lad had been killed at Willaston Club by his electric guitar. He ran all the way home to find Mum gone to hospital having left him a note saying son number two was alive but shocked – well and truly I can assure you.

Eventually I was discharged after two days with only a small burn mark. All seemed well except no one had noticed the burn was deeper than thought and became infected. I spent the next two weeks in bed at home with blood poisoning with doctor's visits twice a day for antibiotic injections. My temperature reached 104 and I became rather delirious. I was about to be re-admitted to the Memorial with twin red lines going up my arm when my temperature broke and I slept for 48 hours. As I write there is still a very faint scar on my finger as a memento of my journey into the realms of Marconi and Farraday.

SUCCESSFUL DEBUT FOR THE DIAMONDS

Philip Rylance (left) and Keith Haines.

TWO guitarists, Philip Rylance and Keith Haines, who have formed a partnership and called themselves "The Diamonds," recently reached a national talent contest area final. They have now passed a B.B.C. broadcasting audition for the North Regional sound programme, and hope they are on the path to fame.

At the audition, these youthful musicians sang two songs they had composed together, and hope to launch their compositions into the "pop" parade in the near future.

Philip, while a scholar at St. Joseph's College, Stoke-on-Trent, was an all-round athlete, with numerous firsts at sprinting, long jump, hurdles and cross-country events. His home is at Richmond-road, Crewe, while his partner, Keith, lives at Broughton-lane, Wistaston.

16

Chapter Three

The Diamonds

After some time Ted and I got itchy feet and decided to try
something different. We decided to become 'The Diamonds',
a dynamic duo featuring popular music of the day! Off we
went to the Oddfellows' Club in Edleston Road and entered a
talent competition. All went well for about four rounds and we
eventually got to the final. This was just about the time when
the Allisons had a huge hit with 'Are You Sure' and dynamic
duos seemed to be the flavour of the month. The night of the
final came and we decided to stick with Buddy Holly and not
become Crewe's Allisons. Had we done the opposite I might
have been writing this from The Bahamas or some other exotic
spot. All the crowd wanted was 'Are You Sure' and we gave
them 'That'll be the Day'. That was it! Game set and match to
Cole Lawrence from Haslington who came up with 'You'll
Never Know'.
'Good as Shirley Bassey any day lad,' was the Oddfellows
opinion of Cole, and the Diamonds slunk off home (on the
bus!) with tails well and truly between legs.

The next day was a school day but Ted and I decided that for
fallen idols school was not a suitable place for wound licking,
so we grabbed girlfriends and skived off to Beeston Castle for
the day. Unbeknown to me St Joseph's was not too pleased
with my musical activities and thus my attendance record and
decided to ring Mama to ascertain the reason for son number

two's absence. Was I ill? Had I a job interview? Had British Rail had some sort of collapse?

'No, no, no,' said Mama, 'he's at school.'

Short telephonic silence......

'Mrs Rylance, if he were at school I would not be ringing,' spluttered one irate Christian Brother.

I still have the mark on my hands if only from the sheer ignominy of being caned at the age of seventeen.

However the Diamonds fared better along other pathways to stardom.

I had begun to work at the local theatre in Crewe, which at that time was the 'New Theatre'. I started round about Christmas 1961 as a stagehand and general dogsbody. It was panto season and that year's show was Babes in the Wood. From the moment I walked backstage I knew what I wanted to do. Here was a world where the only thing that mattered was entertaining the audience. I used to wait by the tabs and feel the excitement as the pit orchestra played the opening bars and the auditorium appeared with a sea of expectant faces. Well the sea was about two rows deep on a wet Tuesday in Crewe, but I was smitten as never before.

The starring comic and later manager of the 'New' was a Halifax comedian called Tony Lester. I got on well with Tony and he was always happy to teach me a few tricks of the trade and fill my head with stories of the good old days of the Glasgow Empire or the Bradford Alhambra. During the six months of my after school work at the theatre it was fascinating to see stars of previous days on their way down from on high coming to Crewe to earn a living. I worked with and helped folks like Ronnie

Carol, Joan Regan, Ruby Murray and Craig Douglas, but the guy who filled the theatre every night for a week was Emile Ford with his Checkmates. With his backing singers and brilliant six piece band they put on a great show and sent the population of Crewe homeward bound each night with a smile on their faces and fingers clicking to 'What do you Wanna Make those Eyes at me for'.

On a Saturday afternoon the theatre was always empty but the place was open for minor repairs or coffee in the foyer. This is when Ted and I used to bring in our guitars, set up on stage and use the house microphone to become stars for about ten minutes. One afternoon some coffee drinkers came into the auditorium and sat listening. Unknown to us they had asked Tony if we were the next week's variety act in for early rehearsal! Well that was it. Tony came and listened and decided that if we were ever going to climb the ladder, the first rung started there and then. He knew an old and well-respected entertainer by the name of Billy Scott-Coomber who was at that time a BBC Radio producer in Manchester. We wrote to Billy explaining what we did and lo and behold we were invited to Manchester for an audition.

After much soul searching about songs to impress producers, we decided to use one of our own and a Ricky Nelson tune offering named 'Lonesome Town'. Our own effort was really Ted's song but I do remember adding one or two Doo-Wops in appropriate places. The great day arrived and off we went (train of course) to a little studio near Piccadilly Station where we did our stuff. Billy Scott-Coomber was a nice old guy and listened carefully and with some enjoyment as we did the best we could with immense nerves jangling throughout our whole beings.

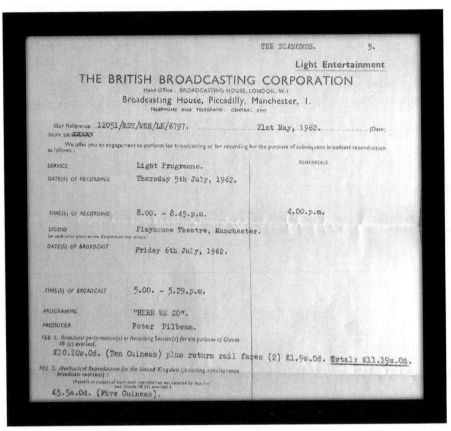

The old BBC second contract for The Diamonds from 1962
10 guineas plus return rail fare – wow!

We were in awe of a real studio with proper equipment and a
real live sound engineer and returned to Crewe convinced that
we had done our best but we would never hear another word.

How wrong can you be! A few days later with wide eyed astonishment I opened a letter from Auntie BBC which contained a contract inviting Messrs Rylance and Haines to attend the old Hippodrome Theatre in Hulme as the Diamonds to record 'Here We Go' for broadcast some three weeks hence. For the next few days we both walked on air thinking that we might wake up and find it all a dream. We practised like mad and I even bought some new strings! Wow... serious stuff.

Recording day arrived and there we were, Crewe Station, platform four, Manchester bound for fame, glory and riches beyond belief, which in fact was the princely sum of ten guineas. Now ten guineas in 1962 was a lot of pocket money even split two ways. On the way there we got the guitars out on the train and entertained some other passengers as we rehearsed our songs. At the theatre rehearsal time found us with Syd Lawrence, Bernard Hermann, Alyn Ainsworth and co who were the famous and fabulous BBC Northern Dance Orchestra or NDO.

'Where's your dots lads?' asked the drummer. 'Dots?'
'Aye, dots, your music, for us to back you on guitar, bass and drums.'
Now here was a thing. Nobody had mentioned backing and we had never heard of dots. So, Harry Archer and Bobby Turner, bass and drums, sat down with us and quickly showed us how to write simple block chords into a page of dots for them to follow. Ted and I retired quietly to the rear of the theatre and in half an hour rushed to the stage with our dots for the two of them to follow. Rehearsal went well and the crucial dots passed inspection without further ado.

The show was being hosted by Roger Moffat who was a big wheel in Northern broadcasting and featured a guy from a four-piece group who had recently gone solo. His name was Val Doonican and he was hoping to make a go of it on his own! He played and sang really well and was a really nice ordinary fella. Anyway, off went the opening music and the show was into full swing. I remember walking onto the stage and seeing a theatre full of what seemed like twelve year old girls. We were introduced and had no time to think of nerves. With dry mouths and butterflies held in check we went into the opening bars of Lonesome Town. If you don't know the song it is a mournful, haunting sort of love song (unrequited), with mostly solo guitar and voice with harmony on the middle eight. After we finished there was a deathly hush, then after a second or two the most fantastic wailing noise of about five hundred young girls screaming and yelling in, we hoped, some sort of appreciation. We had to come back and take a bow as the noise continued, and later Roger Moffat told us it was the longest reception he had ever heard on the show. Wow! We were over the moon and before we knew it were back on stage for our next song, which Ted had written. 'After Thinking It Over' also went down extremely well and we collected another rousing ovation.

At the end of recording we were made a big fuss of by everyone, including the producer Peter Pilbeam. We said our goodbyes and hoped to be coming back for more. As we got outside the theatre we were attacked by a screaming mob of about fifty or sixty young girls. It was quite a strange feeling being pinned up against a wall by a screaming horde all shouting our names. It was only after a few seconds that I felt little hands delving inside my pockets, but could do little about it in the throng. Eventually the fever subsided and Ted and I emerged from the scrum feeling rather sheepish but pleasantly surprised at our first experience of being 'stars'. We took stock of the situation and found that about four shillings and seven pence had been neatly lifted from our combined persons leaving us with not a lot to return home with. I wondered how the girls fared with The Beatles who had been the previous week's guests. I often smile and ask myself if a Beatle four and seven pence was worth more than a Diamonds four and seven pence! Or was Paul McCartney pinned up against the same wall as yours truly in Hulme, Manchester?

On the way back to Crewe on the train we wrote another song and believe it or not performed this very song on our next appearance on 'Here We Go'. Oh yes the good old BBC sent us another contract the very next day. We were thrilled and could see the stars twinkling before our eyes. Where were we bound for, how many hits would we have, would we have a chauffeur as we were too young to drive, how deep would the swimming pool be at the deep end!

To quote Charles Dickens, 'What larks we would have, what larks'.

Chapter Four
Hot Rod Days

Majestic Ballroom Crewe 1962

The Iron Door   Liverpool 1962

Ted had dropped a bit of a bombshell in the late days of 1961 by saying he had been asked to join the Hot Rods and was going to take up the offer. To say I was stunned was an understatement, to say the least. We made great music as a duo and the guys in the Echoes were our mates. What would I tell them? What would they think? Was this the end of life as I knew it? In the end it all fizzled out and the Echoes became a part of history never to see the light of day again. As for the Diamonds duo, can you believe that I actually wrote to the BBC saying that we didn't want any more work thank you very much! Now there were people in this business who would kill for a radio audition, and there we were, having had two highly successful shows and promises of more, spurning offers of even more and better work. Mad or what!

Anyway off Ted went and I was like a dog who'd lost his bone. I didn't play, I didn't want to play I couldn't stand the thought of playing the guitar. So what do you do when you can't or won't play guitar – you play the drums. In my case this was a bit awkward because I didn't have any drums and if I did I couldn't play. Interesting! Ted to the rescue; he came round saying that The Rods drummer was rather unreliable and sometimes let them down at the last minute, did I fancy the job? I laughed until he told me that he was serious and if I could get some drums he would teach me to play; clever lad our Ted. It's surprising the strange looks you get when you sit in the Crosville bus station café and practise drums with a knife, fork, three plates and a glazed look in your eye. The two of us sat for hours after school when our buses would meet, mine from Crewe station, Ted's from Sandbach where he was at school. He started to teach me the basic rock rhythm to songs like Diana and The Girl of My Best Friend. I can remember getting hopelessly aggravated because my fingers would not do what my brain was commanding. The basic eight in the bar with the right hand on the high-hat (dinner plate) and bang the left hand fork on the side plate on the third, fourth and seventh beat. Easy really. I beg you dear reader to go into your local café and try this out. You will be amazed at the response, especially if you sing Diana with your lip curled up at the side!

Now I ask you, what are mums and dads for? Mine had nothing in the bank, lived in a rented house and scrimped and saved to provide me and my brother with a decent upbringing. From where, I know not, but £25 appeared to enable me to go to Hanley one Saturday morning and purchase an Olympic drum kit in silver pearl. I was in ecstasy and travelled back in the Hot Rods van surrounded by silver pearl and two cymbals. Howard Lynch, the Rods bass player, had driven me there and laughed all the way back to Crewe at the sight of me in his rear view mirror trying to play the drums in the back of an old Morris Commercial Post Office van.

The stage was set for my drumming career to begin in earnest. I put the kit up in the front room at Richmond Road because ours was a northern house and the front room was only used for Christmas, funerals and important visitors. I bashed and sang, sang and bashed, crashed and rolled till eventually I thought it sounded at least reasonable. After one week the big day arrived. The Hot Rods had a gig at a youth club right in the middle of Oulton Park racetrack near Tarporley. I set up trying to look confident with Ted offering help, advice and moral fortitude. A pint or two of Greenall Whitley's best bitter would have done the trick but it was a youth club after all. Before I knew it we had started with our sort of signature tune, Johnny B Goode from the king of them all - Chuck Berry. Every chorus the guitar lads would kick their legs in the air on the word 'GO' and I was supposed to crash the main cymbal. I nearly got them tripped up over their own legs a few times but at the end of that song all the girls yelled for more and a few of the lads clapped. Success.

Believe it or not the gig went well and I was in. I was a Hot Rod, something that every aspiring musician in Crewe would give their right arm to be.

This was late sixty-one and early sixty-two and the Liverpool boom was just about to be born. Rumours abounded of a group of four guys who were scruffy, had lousy equipment, played their own songs and had no lead singer or echo chamber. Wow! How could this be? And to cap it all they had a stupid name – The Beatles. Now I ask you who on earth would ever think of trying to make a career in the Rock'n'Roll business with that name – pause for reflection!!! At that time Liverpool was a strange place to play because each band had its own followers who would trek miles to see their favourites at each and every gig. If you had a favourite band then that was it. You followed them and virtually no others. Some of the good bands from the city that come to mind are as follows, Mark Peters and the Silhouettes from Litherland Town Hall, Earl Royce and the Olympics, Faron's Flamingoes, with the incredible Trevor Morais on drums, Denny Seyton and the Sabres, The Undertakers, the Big Three with the brilliant Brian

Griffiths on guitar and of course Mr Liverpool, Rory Storm and the Hurricanes. Now tucked away in amongst this mass of talented bands were The Beatles. Original, clever, funny, greatly talented, single minded, and mind blowing! It didn't take fans long to realise that here was something different. Like the other bands The Beatles had their own faithful followers who soon began to outnumber all the rest of the local groups. Their fans were always dressed in full black, nearly always trousers for the girls, longish hair for the guys and often strange smelling cigarettes. They were often thought of as Art-School types and Beat Generation, straight from a Jack Kerouac novel. This was all very different to any other city and it was the scene which we entered in 1961.

Eventually we were booked to do the Iron Door Club in Temple Street, just off Dale Street. The Beatles were to do every Sunday and alternate Sundays their support group would be The Hot Rods or Billy Kramer and the Coasters, not yet Billy J Kramer and the Dakotas!! This was to last for about two months. We did the first gig and my mind was blown apart by something I had never ever seen or heard before. The music of the Beatles was simply stunning and amazing. Sheer excitement and aggression with no pause for breath. There were no hit parade numbers from Cliff and the Shadows or no Ricky Nelson or Paul Anka. Instead we got James Rae, Chan Romero, Arthur Alexander and other obscure American singers. Strangely enough there were no Lennon McCartney songs at all, but what a performance. So much electric energy in one band it was just incredible. We all got on well in the dressing room, except for Pete Best who was always somewhere else with a load of girls in tow, and agreed to meet up again in two weeks.

We were not to know but tragedy was about to strike in the cruellest of ways. Ray Jones one of our singers was an avid shotgun enthusiast and he and his friend Keith used to go over to Crewe Hall fields every Sunday after wood pigeons and rabbits. This particular Sunday was a Beatles Sunday at the Iron Door. At about mid-day a knock on the door signalled the arrival of Garry and Howard Lynch. 'We won't be going tonight,' Lynchie said. 'Ray's been in an accident.' Ray was a biker with a 500cc Bonneville so I immediately thought, traffic accident. But no, poor Ray had jumped over a style in front of his friend Keith who jumped over after him. Keith's gun was loaded and accidentally fired as he jumped down off the style. The twelve bore cartridge could have gone anywhere in the Cheshire countryside. But it was not to be. Ray died almost instantly from a horrific wound to the rear of his skull. Mercifully he would never have known anything about it. Words cannot and never will be able to describe the feelings of the band. We were just obliterated – smashed – ruined in one moment of fateful madness. The thing I will always remember is my Dad in floods of tears. He hardly knew Ray but he could see what his son and friends were going through.... a good man my Dad.

Chapter Five

A Professional Entertainer!

About mid 1962 I took my A levels in French, History and English. I had not burnt the midnight oil in studying except of the guitar-playing kind of study in the pubs and clubs of the North West. I was still a Hot Rod and enjoying the kudos of the position as rhythm guitar player and second singer. My drumming had been found to be not up to scratch and I was replaced by Dave Heaps, another Rolls Royce apprentice who was very good indeed for a sixteen year old. He was a natural and had been home taught by his brother Mick, another former Hot Rod, who had been a drummer in one of the army regimental bands.

At that time Tommy Bruce who had had chart hits with Ain't Misbehavin' and Buttons and Bows was looking for a band to become his Bruisers when he toured the North of England on one – nighters. The bass player's sister was the secretary of his fan club so guess who got the job? The Hot Rods and the Bruisers became one and the same and we started much more serious work in places like Halifax Victoria Hall for Shirley Crabtree (Big Daddy the wrestler), Prestatyn Lido, Ashton in Makerfield, Liverpool, Manchester, and many more. Getting in at three in the morning from a gig is not conducive to understanding the finer points of Chaucer and Victor Hugo and thus the schoolwork suffered accordingly. I was still playing rugby for the school and contrived to be injured just about every other game so that I could have Monday and Tuesday off with ankle ligament trouble. This would give me time to get over a long weekend with the guitar in far-flung places, like Wavertree Youth Club and Rotherham Baths.

Tommy used to start his act with Great Balls of Fire. We would do two numbers as a warm up and then turn our backs on the crowd. He would rush onto the stage shouting, 'Fire! Fire! Great balls of fire.' On the words fire the guitar players would turn round to face the audience and we all played a loud chord of C. Ted was supposed to turn first. Now Ted used to get carried away with thinking and at times seemed to be in his own little world. At the Halifax Vic in front of a very large crowd, poor old Tom rushed onto the stage shouting 'Fire' at the top of his voice. No reaction from Ted! 'Fire' shouts Tom – no reaction. Again 'Fire' - Ted was miles away obviously deep in thought. Eventually Tom shouted 'Ted there's a bloody fire in here,' to which I turned round closely followed by Ted. 'Oh' said Ted later in the dressing room, 'I'd forgotten I was first. It was because I was wearing my sunglasses!' To this day I know not why!!!

If I have one great regret about all of this it is the fact that I was letting my Mum and Dad down – bigtime! They had no money, nobody in Crewe Works had any money in those days, and they had scrimped and saved to put me through sixth form. Looking back on it now I am very sad about what happened and sometimes long to be able to put the clock back to try to make some sort of amends. But you can't go back - ever. It all came to a head in the late summer of '62. In those days the Staffordshire Evening Sentinel published A- level results about six weeks after the exams were taken by candidates. I had duly taken my three but was not happy with my performance in any. I was predicted a good pass in French and passes in the other two. I rushed out to buy the Sentinel and eagerly scanned the St. Joseph's results. The names were listed in alphabetical order and there was a huge gap between P and S. Shock – Horror – Sickness –Panic – Unbelievability. The thoughts that ran through my head included getting drunk before I went home, not going home – ever - jumping under the Midday Scott, running away to sea. In the end I plucked up courage and slunk off down Prince Albert Street, Earle Street and Richmond Road to number 120. Both there – no shouting – no sound – no tears just a horrible sad look of disappointment and hurt like I had never seen before. We were all three of us speechless. If any tears were to come they would have come from me. Dad went to put the kettle on, Mum just looked and I felt absolutely bloody awful. These two good and lovely people had just about put everything on the line for me and I had repaid them like this. Eventually I decided that there was no going back and thus forward was the only way.

'Now I'll have to become a singer won't I with no qualifications. I'm not doing a third year sixth form and I'm not going on the railway.'

After a while of sulking and licking wounds I eventually decided to contact Tony Lester who had moved on from Crewe Theatre. We arranged to meet in Blackpool and he gave me the address of an agent friend of his named Jack Webb. Jack was one of a group of agents throughout the north of UK who had formed the BPA, Beat Promoters Association, with the idea that each one of them would take an act, say Johnny Kidd, and find him five days' work in his area before passing him over to the next agent's area. Some of the names were, I think, Peter Walsh in London, John Singer in Birmingham, Jack Webb in northern England, Danny Betesh in Manchester (later to become a very big name in Beatles history) and the infamous Duncan McKinnon in the Scottish Borders. Drunken Duncan, as he was known, controlled Lockerbie, Annan, Melrose, Kelso, and Galashiels etc.

I met Jack who lived in North Blackpool and he found me a job whilst trying to fix me up with a band to sing with. I proudly became a bingo caller and money collector for HM's Bingo, which was the very first one on the Golden Mile after Central Pier where the Mile started. It was right next to Madame Tussauds and always attracted loads of customers. I worked from nine am to nine pm every day for twelve pounds a week. WOW!! That was good money in those days, but very tiring. I remember my first week I blew seven pounds of it on a shiny new fleece lined leather jacket. I sold it to my cousin from The Scorpions eight years later for five pounds!

I found lodgings with a fierce old lady called Mrs Brickwood just behind Central Pier. She and her daughter Maud ran a five storey boarding house which had an attic for three pounds a week bed and breakfast. The arrangement was I could have the room but when the house was full I had to share the attic with other likeminded young guys who were broke. It all worked well and I met some great lads from London, Glasgow and Nottingham. Maud's breakfasts were substantial enough for me to be able to manage till my hour off for my next meal. When nine-o-clock came I went off to the pub with new mates from various parts of the country.

As far as the singing went Jack was trying to find me work and
I started to do spots at his dance at the Marine Hall in
Fleetwood. One of the bands I sang with was the Manchester
Playboys who were to go off to Hamburg for September and
October. Jack fixed it that I would go as their singer as the
wages were per man not per band. We were to get twenty five
pounds per man per week and lodgings found. For 1962 that
was really great money and so I jumped at the chance. My
passport was sorted and I eagerly awaited being picked up in
the group van for the start of my meteoric career in the world
of pop. Not so fast! The day came, and the next, and the next
and I was still in Blackpool with Mrs Brickwood and Maud.
Now there was nothing wrong Mrs B and Maud but they did
not have the same attraction for a would-be star as the lights of
Hamburg and The Reeperbahn – and still I waited. Eventually
I discovered the band had gone without me. I still don't know
why this happened but I was distraught and heartbroken. What
could I do? I suppose I could improve my bingo calling and
try for a job with Mecca. I could stay on with Jack and get a
few singing jobs. I could try bar work in Blackpool which was
plentiful.

It was now early September and I rang my Mum, as you do.
She told me that The Crescents, a local Crewe group, were
about to turn professional with a contract to back Susan Singer
who was Helen Shapiro's cousin. Their singer and rhythm
player, Pat Withers, was leaving as he had a wife and family
and needed a weekly secure wage. I needed no more telling. I
resigned from HM's bingo and got the train to Crewe two days
later. Harry Myers who was a hard but fair old guy, paid me
up to date and wished me well. His wife said I should visit

34

when I was a star and come and see them in a Rolls Royce (from Crewe of course). This was the beginning – stardom was at hand. I could feel it in my bones. Watch out world here I come!

Chapter Six

Phil Ryan and the Crescents

PHIL RYAN and the CRESCENTS

Phil Ryan – vocals and sort of rhythm guitar
Bernie Hibbert – guitar
Dave Birkenhead - bass
Roger Keay – drums and tenor sax

Phil Rylance (right) and The Crescents.

A very old cutting of the first Phil Ryan and the Crescents

Ken Lockwood - bass guitar
Keith Billington - drums
Bernie Hibbert – guitar
Phil Ryan – vocals

Bernard and Roger, both aged about seventeen, on guitar and tenor sax with Roger's Dad's band, The Keynotes. Probably Crewe Corn Exchange in the late fifties.

This was just about the time when small dance bands were giving way to 'beat groups' with electric gear.

I remember meeting up with Bernard at 167 Middlewich Street, which became known as the 167 Club; a meeting place for musicians' recreation! We talked and talked and he showed me the plans for The Crescents in the near future with work in Stoke on Trent, Manchester and then the Susan Singer tour. It all looked good and we agreed that as from then on it would be Phil Ryan and the Crescents. We set to work rehearsing with Steve Jenks on bass and Keith Billington on drums. It all went surprisingly well and we sounded pretty good for a new small outfit. Bernard played a Hofner Verithin and as the only guitarist had to play a sort of lead come rhythm at the same time. He was an excellent reader and his playing really filled out any gaps. Steve Jenks was another good musician and had a beautiful Fender Precision Bass which sounded great. Keith was a solid drummer with a good kit. All was set for us to dive into showbiz full time.

My Mum made me two shirts to play in; one blue satin and the other silver glitter. Can you imagine it? I ordered a pair of white leather Chelsea boots from Jack Gresty, the manager of the Co-op shoe department. The outfit was completed by a pair of black very tight trousers which copied Billy Fury, whom I'd gigged with at Crewe Town Hall previously.

All was set for the first gig at Tarporley Cinema late September 1962. We were using two Vox AC 30 twins with a Leak 25 Watt PA and two Reslo mikes. Looking back it all sounds extremely small stuff but in those days we were reasonably well equipped. The gear was checked, rehearsal was finished and we were ready for the off.

Chapter Seven

September 1962

First gig – Tarporley Cinema for a nice old guy called Mr Fennel. Blue silk shirt-tight black trousers and white Chelsea boots! Two sets - band played three openers then introduced me. Girls crowded around front of low stage. First song – 'Fabulous' (Charlie Gracie) then 'Bona Serra' (Conway Twitty). Two sets went well – rebooked for three months. Went home with adrenalin pumping.

Three pubs in Stoke on Trent the next week – Wagon and Horses, Meir (right where the tunnel under the A50 is now), The Hempstalls Lane Inn and The Hollybush in Blurton. All three were for an agent named Keith Fisher who managed the Marauders who were to later get into the charts with 'That's what I Want' and then toured with the Beatles.

In the autumn of 1962 Steve Jenks, bass man, decided he didn't want to give up the day job for the insecurity of pop fame and fortune! So we were joined by Ken Lockwood on bass guitar. Ken was a wizard on lead guitar riffs but was a better cricketer than bass guitar player! However the die was cast and off we went.

We started a three-week tour as backing band for Susan Singer (Helen Shapiro's cousin), with rehearsals at Alsager Youth Club with her producer, Jeff Baker (big noise in the business!). Alsager was also the first gig of the tour.

All went well with guitar player Bernard, a good reader and musician, carrying us all through with his expertise. I was playing a Futurama 2 with great sound but horrible action – sore fingers. Some of Susie's songs were difficult – e.g. Autumn Leaves in B flat!

Next step of tour - Rotherham Baths – rolled up early - wrong date! Next week! This was for Jack Webb the Blackpool agent who had been involved in my aborted German tour. Jack's mix-up once more. This was not our fault and we never ever saw Rotherham Baths again. Called at big hotel near Buxton on way home – refused entry – leather jackets and scruffy jeans – found fish and chip shop –one shilling (five pence) for fish and chips – heaven!

The Three Coins Manchester was a big gig with Susie, Susan Maughan and Freddie and the Dreamers appeared as well. Freddie very funny. Next day we were off to Scotland for more of the tour, about a week for Duncan McKinnon in the Borders. Kelso Corn Exchange – we played top of the bill to the Alex Harvey Soulband – fabulous band and sound – seven piece with two tenor saxes. We were later to meet Alex Harvey in the Top Ten Club in Hamburg where he was a big star. At Kelso we met a great guy called Bob Harkness who asked if the band, when we finished the tour with Susie, would come and play for him at Gretna Green Stormont Hall. More of that later, but Gretna Green was to become our saviour when there was no local work around Cheshire.

We did Whitburn Miner's Welfare with Johnny Kidd and the Pirates – what a sound for three guys, Mick Green on guitar, who was later to star with Tom Jones in the States for years,

Frank Farley was on drums and Johnny Spence on bass. The place was full as in those days all pubs were closed in Scotland on a Sunday so clubs and welfares were always full and put on good bands and shows. Like lots of places in Scotland, pies were provided for the bands during the interval. In Whitburn they had a guy called Fat Jimmy who obviously had a liking for pies by the look of his waistline. Jimmy was the caretaker of the hall and during the bands performance the number of warm pies seemed to get smaller and smaller at each look in the oven. Eventually there were about three pies left out of about a dozen for both bands. One memory I will take to my grave is of a very irate Johnny Kidd, complete with pirate cutlass, holding a spluttering Fat Jimmy up against the wall saying in his lovely cockney accent, 'Ere Jimmy, you've eaten all the pies you fat bastard.'

I often wonder if this is where the football chant started. About half an hour later Fat Jimmy reappeared with half a dozen pies and tried to placate Johnny who looked a fearsome sight in his pirate outfit complete with sword which Jimmy was eyeing with extreme caution.

Susie stayed at our house in Crewe for the length of the tour and we used to stay up late rehearsing duo songs in case music hall ever made a comeback! We did a real mean version of Side by Side, a bit like Max Bygraves meets Dolly Parton! I'm sure we could have got gigs on Worker's Playtime or Music While you Work on the old steam radio!
For those readers who don't remember the aforementioned programmes, they were both wartime based nonstop music shows. For those of you who do remember I hope you're enjoying your Horlicks and keeping up with the Deep Heat!

Eventually the tour came to an end with Susie back to London leaving us a bit apprehensive as to where the work would be coming from. We started the hard slog of finding gigs for the winter. Luckily the pubs and working men's clubs were thriving with full employment in the towns and factories and most cities had four or five nights of live entertainment venues on the go at all times. Stoke-on-Trent was our nearest city and we started to work for Keith Fisher more and more as the venues seemed to like our sort of style. At this time Bernard moved on to piano and small keyboard and we welcomed Steve Jenks back to the group. Steve had had a long face since we went on the road without him because he chose to stay in safe employment with British Rail in their Crewe Office.

In those days a band could earn a living from their music and become 'pro musicians'. Standards varied greatly but the reason for so many pro bands was that every church hall, village hall and working men's club had a regular dance or concert night. If you just played pops you were limited but the Crescents were very versatile and were equally at home doing teenage dances, masonic ladies nights, club nights, youth clubs and factory parties. We could and would play any type of music that people wanted. This stood us in good stead as a regular working band. I remember one week in early 1963 doing Tuesday, Wednesday and Thursday in Stoke pubs, Friday in a Crewe youth club, Saturday at the Plaza in Old Hill, Birmingham and Sunday in Sheffield at another club.

A word about wages - the smallest gig was £8 per night and the biggest £25 in 1963. The Stoke pubs paid about a tenner per band in the week. Working men's clubs paid £15 to £18 but the high spots at the time were Sheffield clubs which paid about £25. Now petrol was 5 shillings (25p) per gallon, so going to Stoke for a tenner left us about £2 each after expenses. Most guys were working for £2 per day in those days so in a good week we were not doing too badly!

Who shot Winco Billington?

To liven up our travels and bring a bit of fun to the proceedings we all decided to buy air guns. Off we went to Wooldridges which was the local iron mongers and hardware store and came out carrying an assortment of BSA Airsporter 22 rifles. We were travelling a lot and used to set off early on many mornings which left us plenty of time to stop on the way and find some secluded wood or fields to practise our new hobby.

One particular day we were off to Scotland to do a weekend in the Borders and were not due to book into our digs until about five pm. In those days the M6 was virtually non-existent so it was the A49 to Haydock then the A6 all the way up to the Scottish border. Before the grind of travelling over Shap Fell on the old road we decided to stop just north of Kendal and do some exploring. Off we went into a roadside wood to try our new toys. We were doing quite well with our impressions of Gary Cooper and John Wayne, by setting up tin cans on fences and pretending they were the Clanton gang at the OK Corral. After twenty minutes of this we decided to track off through the woods with weapons at the ready prepared to ward off any marauding Vikings or pillaging Norsemen.

Earlier in the year we had decided we needed to get warm gear for the winters on the road so we had all bought flying jackets with proper sheepskin linings. Keith, the drummer, bought a huge expensive jacket and was immediately christened Winco, after many RAF heroes of wartime movies.

'I know what,' said Winco, 'let's see how powerful the airguns are. I'll go on ahead and sit down on the path and you can shoot pellets into my back and see how good my coat is as protection.' I ask you. How daft can you get?

'Good idea,' we all chorused. So off Keith went till he reached a clear bit in the path where he squatted down and pulled his sheepskin up over his head to avoid any nasty accidents! 'OK, ready,' came a thin and weedy voice from under the pulled up collar of the thick, furry coat.

'Right. Here we go,' was the reply. We took aim from about twenty five yards away. 'FIRE.' All of a sudden there was a sort of strangulated scream from Winco and this figure leapt about five feet into the air and ran like hell whilst trying to rip his coat off and rub his back at the same time. Eventually we caught up with him and inspected the damage to his frame. There were three red marks indented in his skin, all closely grouped to show the skill of the shooting party! 'Bloody hell, that hurt,' was the first comment that came from the target as he rubbed and rubbed to try to get rid of the marks and the stinging sensation. Needless to say no one else took up the position of target on that day or forever more in the history of the band.

I recently saw Keith at the funeral of a mutual friend. 'How's the back?' I asked. 'Still bloody sore after fifty four years,' came the reply with a grin. Ah well! You never grow up really do you?

About this time Jo Meek had discovered The Tornadoes and given them a massive hit with Telstar. We gigged with them at Shrewsbury Music Hall and were suitably knocked out by Alan Caddy, Clem Cattini, Johnny Spence and co. The new man was Heinz Burt who was a lovely looking chap, but he couldn't play or sing! However they had a fantastic reception from the crowd and Heinz wowed the girls.

The tune of Telstar was played on a Clavioline so we decided to go along this route. We bought a Univox, I think, which was more versatile than a Clav and changed our repertoire to include everything with a keyboard sound. We used to mic up the pianos from each gig we played and sounded quite reasonable as a sort of Jerry lee Lewis meets Rolf Harris. Unfortunately in those days pianos in pubs were somewhat neglected and never tuned. Poor Bernard used to arrive at the stage to be met by an old upright which was just about one tone down from concert pitch. The Univox would not detune that low so at some gigs Bernard would play in D with his left hand and C with his right on the Univox. After about one hour of this he used to say, 'My head hurts.'

About this time we started to gig a lot in Birmingham and Wolverhampton for the Astra Agency who had a band called the N'Betweens. We got on well with them and we always looked forward to gigs together as a sort of brotherhood of the road. This used to exist a lot in those days and we would be good mates with bands in different areas. I well remember we all used to stand on the side of the stage and watch each other's set from the wings. Sometimes other band members would join in. One that comes to mind was Mike Pinder from the Moody Blues who sat in with us at a pub gig in South Birmingham. He wasn't gigging so he came along and joined in the band. There were the N'Betweens from Wolverhampton, The Liberators from Rugby, The Delmonts from Liverpool, The Dakotas from Manchester, The Idle Race from Birmingham and many others. The N'Betweens changed their name to Slade, The Liberators became Pinkertons Assorted Colours, The Dakotas went with Billy Ashton (Billy J Kramer), and The Idle Race became The Move. Denny Lane and the Diplomats were an up and coming Midlands band who we worked with a lot and suddenly found them having a massive hit with 'Go Now' as the Moody Blues. Denny later joined Wings with my coke drinking friend from The Iron Door (see preface).

Phil Ryan and The Crescents

Published by Combo Publications

An early publicity shot
The band at The Roaches near Leek

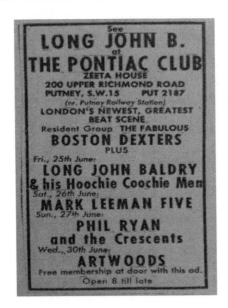

We had met a nice old Scottish chap in Kelso, name of Bob Harkness, who we contacted and told him we were free now to play Gretna Green on a Friday night. Little did we know that he was to be our saviour for many years to come when work in England was scarce. Bernard quoted Bob twenty five pounds for the night and to our surprise that was accepted without any problem at all.

Now £25 doesn't sound a lot these days for four guys. However look at the figures and you will see that this sort of money was a lifeline to a group trying to make a go of it and break into the world of showbiz! The gig was a three hundred miles round trip. Petrol was three shillings and eleven pence per gallon (19 and a half pence in today's money) which equates to about 4 and a half pence per litre. The van did about 25 mpg, thus total fuel cost for the trip was around today's equivalent of £2.50. Allowing for meals we still came out of the one gig with £20 to split four/five ways. If we were lucky and got a three night weekend it was really good money even with 10% agents fees to pay for some of the gigs. For a group like us that was top rate. In those days you could book Georgie Fame, Johnny Kidd, Screamin' Lord Sutch etc for a midweek gig for about forty or fifty quid, so you can see we were doing OK with our Scottish travels.

Christmas 1962 came and went with all the usual type of gigs, The Cosy Club, Haslington, Crewe Coppenhall Club, Nantwich Civic Hall. We tried to keep reasonably local for obvious reasons of travel and weather. All went well until the big freeze of 1963 which came in January. We set off one Sunday morning to do Rotherham Working Men's club which was always known as 'Tanic - short for Titanic. Why I do not know but it was! Anyway we reached Macclesfield and set off over the tops to get to Chapel-en-le-Frith via Kettleshulme. This was our usual route to Sheffield which brought us in over Mam Tor in the Peaks and then into the city via Abbeydale. About three miles out of Macc we had a strange experience; the road just disappeared. We were driving along in about a foot of snow when we were confronted by a wall of about eight feet of the white stuff right across the road in front of us. It was just invisible until about ten yards away when we came to a slow and skidded halt. What shall we do now thought four musical brains? 'Where are we now-my love' was the musical answer. A quick turnaround was the order of the day and a thirty mile detour via south Manchester and the moors, which luckily had been cleared. Anyway we arrived in Rotherham and knocked on the backdoor of 'Tanic. A guy of about six feet five with muscles in his eyebrows and scars to match popped his head out and uttered the unforgettable words 'You're a bit late love.' Now coming from Crewe if you called another guy love you were either his Dad or his sleeping partner complete with pink shirt and tight trousers! This guy was dead serious and an ex rugby league player - come- miner who was a club member. It wasn't till months later that we became accustomed to the 'love' between tough heterosexual adult males. Anyway the gig must have gone well as were re-booked for later in the year.

The year carried on and we proudly boast that we didn't lose any gigs to the snow. The only casualty to the weather in our whole career was a gig with Susan Singer at Middlesbrough

Majestic (or Locarno). We got as far as Leeds in a monster pea-soup fog. A guy rolled back into us in Rochdale and got out of his car playing hell that we had rolled forward into him! He was eventually smoothed over and we carried on into the murk. Seven o'clock came and we all realised that Middlesbrough at this rate would arrive at something like five in the morning. What to do – cheap bed and breakfast. We found a Jewish private hotel where the boss welcomed Suzie with open arms, she being of the chosen faith. We booked in and I shivered the way through the night with the start of bronchitis and flu. Morning arrived and the hotelier informed Suzie that he had some nice kosher bacon which he would cook for her. However when she found it was dearer than ordinary bacon we all had ordinary! Ah happy days.

Chapter Eight

The First Break-up

Round about this time we asked a good friend of ours to join as manager cum road manager cum general advisor/helper in every way possible. Derek Hughes was an extremely capable guy who could turn his hand to most things mechanical and electrical. He was another of Rolls Royce's apprentices who went on to more interesting things. He gave up his day job and came to live with my Mum and Dad in Richmond Road, Crewe. His own Mum and Dad had just left the Brunswick to go to North Manchester to manage the Clough Hotel not far off the Oldham Road. I well remember after gigs sitting up with Derek quaffing endless cups of tea and talking about American cars and bands. Money was tight so tea from Mum's tea caddy was the cheapest option. Derek was great at building and mending, and lots of our equipment was courtesy of the Hughes Corporation! This arrangement carried on until the spring of 1963 when things began to become a bit different and relationships in the band became strained; nothing to do with Derek at all. The end of this band was in sight and Derek eventually left and went to work in Manchester I think. I will never forget the next time we met. I was walking up Edleston Road and who should pull up at the traffic lights but Derek. He called me over and said 'Shake hands with Billy J Kramer's new road manager.' Wow. Great news and a great opportunity for Derek. We kept in touch and got many postcards from

New York, Stockholm, Sydney and other far off exotic places. Well done Derek you deserved all of it.

A very early picture of Derek Hughes, far left, also with Ray Jones of the Hot Rods.

In the early spring of 1963 we realised that all was not well, not so much with the playing but with the social side of the band. Living in close proximity to the same guys, day in and day out, soon takes its toll and shows up cracks in the wallpaper. Somehow the situation seemed to develop into me and Bernie as a group and the others, Ken, Keith and Steve, as a sort of other part of the band. We had taken on a new manager who was a local guy called John Edgley. He and his family started to run the Crewe Town Hall dances and fancied themselves as entrepreneurs of the Epstein type. To put it bluntly they had not a clue!! Full of big ideas and a plan to conquer the world of showbiz. However the world of showbiz did not want to be conquered by the Edgleys and the arrangement was rather short lived. Things came to a head during the summer and gigs did not go well, bookings were cancelled and generally life was poor for a wannabe pop star! We met at a friend's, Derek Evanson's house in Evans Street Crewe, to 'clear the air' and after a short and rather volatile meeting we nearly came to blows. Luckily that didn't happen but the end was in sight. Bernie and I went home, the others stayed and the upshot was - no more Phil Ryan and the Crescents.... or so it seemed at that time. What could I do?

I got in touch with Tony Lester from Crewe Theatre and he readily agreed to try and help. He was touring with a summer review show of Snow White and the Seven Dwarfs. I joined the cast at Oxford New Theatre and was a general dogsbody trying to help out where I could. In the show were a couple called Roy and Billie Barber. Roy was a stilt-walker, acrobat and general cabaret artist. Billie, his wife, was the sister of Sheila Hancock, the actress. They were a great couple and always had a good word for me. Unfortunately one day Roy got his stilt caught in the revolving stage at the theatre and fell headlong onto the stage floor from about fifteen feet high. A nasty injury meant hospital treatment and forbidden from driving. The show was to move to the Alhambra, Morecambe, the next week, so guess who got the job of driving Roy and Billie to Morecambe. They lived in Switzerland and did lots of European work in cabaret and circus and were thus entitled to buy a new tax free car each year from a foreign country. When I stepped out of the digs to see their car, in front of me was a gleaming brand new Mercedes 200 fin tail saloon. Wow Wow Wow!!!

'You can drive an automatic?' asked Billie. 'Left hand drive as well?'

'Yeah – course I can.' Ulp Ulp Ulp!! I don't know what Ulp really means but I remember seeing Desperate Dan looking really bemused with an 'Ulp' bubble above his head in the Dandy. And boy was I bemused!!

Well we set off and I was trying to change gear for about ten miles! We were in convoy to travel - the Mercedes, Tony Lester's Wolseley 4/44 and an old Renault belonging to a comic called Tony Hughes, who was I think The King of the Castle in the show. This was just the time when the M6 was being built very near to Crewe. 'I know the way,' I piped up and led the convoy off the main A34 towards the villages of Alsager, Betchton and eventually Sandbach. Little did I realise that this was the main Wimpy/McAlpine through route for works traffic. Ulp! Again! Now a brand new Mercedes is a lovely vehicle but is no match for a thirty ton Euclid surface scraper or a D8 Caterpillar Bulldozer. Well! I didn't actually hit anything, but Roy and Billie cowered in the passenger seats as their beloved mode of transport ploughed through ten inches deep mud puddles and over lumps and stones from the diggings. 'Interesting route,' was the response when we arrived in Morecambe later that day. 'Sure the A34 wouldn't have been quicker?' What can you say? 'Perhaps so,' I agreed, 'but you would have missed out on some breath-taking elements of the Cheshire countryside.'

Once ensconced in Morecambe I started work at the Alhambra as a sort of theatre assistant working nine am till ten at night. Long hours but I was in the theatre business and I loved it. The summer show was the Hughie Green show, a sort of spin off from his TV series Double Your Money. Kenny Lynch was also in the show and Sheila Southern together with a duo of polish piano players named Rawicz and Landauer (that'll test your memory dear reader). It was a sell out every night. The strange thing was Hughie Green arrived at the theatre at 8.30, went onstage at 8.45, came off at about 10 o'clock and left through the stage door. He never spoke a word to anybody, ever, except his manager, Vic Hallums. Backstage I was put in charge of working the echo unit for the vocals for Kenny and Sheila. I was the only one who knew how it worked as I had one exactly the same with The Crescents. It was a Klempt Echolette, a very expensive German piece of kit in those days. All was well except for one night when I was distracted and Kenny's announcements sounded like the voice on platform seven of Crewe station. I was supposed to turn the echo to zero for any speech before the next song. Luckily he thought it was funny or I would have had the world's shortest career as an echo chamber operator!

During the afternoon I used to go along to the Winter Gardens and got to know the resident group, a four piece from Liverpool called The Sabres, I think. I used to get up and sing with them and soon realised that the pull of singing on stage was greater than being a stagehand and twiddling echo chamber knobs.

Eventually The Alhambra and I parted company. The season was coming to an end and Hughie Green was off to pastures new. What next, I hear you say. Well I returned to Crewe in September 63 to find all the Liverpool bands with whom we had played at the cavern and the Iron Door had got great

56

recording contracts whilst we had split up and gone our different ways.

The Beatles led the charge with Love Me Do. Then along came Gerry with How Do You Do It, Billy J with Secret, The Searchers with Sweets for my Sweet, The Fourmost with Hello Little Girl etc etc etc. This was, to say the least, most galling, as we had played alongside them all and had topped the bill to most except the Fab Four! Where to go now? Answer – re-join The Crescents. Bernie had carried on the name with two new guys; Roger Keay and Dave Birkenhead. All three were good gigging musicians and had a tight sound for a three piece. They were working well and doing a lot of Scottish gigs for good money split three ways. I still got on well with Bernie and went with them to a gig they were doing at the 76 club in Burton on Trent. The club owner was a guy called Gordon Hand (or Band) who seemed to like the group. They were doing all the sixties Liverpool stuff and I eventually got up on stage and did Saw Her Standing There and Twist and Shout. The reception was very good with the crowd well pleased, as was Mr Hand (Band). There was only one thing for it. Phil Ryan and the Crescents – mark two!!!

We set about rehearsing hard and eventually produced a sound and quality which was about the best I had ever had with any previous band. The gigs were pretty much the same as before with the added attraction of quite a few Scottish weekends. We made lots of good friends up there and made sure we were always polite, pleasant and punctual - easy to say but not always obvious to a lot of bands. Most of the Scottish work was in the Borders with names like Lockerbie, Langholm, Newton Stewart, Hawick, Galashiels and our staple diet of

Gretna Green Stormont Hall. We did the Stormont for Bob Harkness about ten times a year and made many good friends among the local folk. An interesting scenario at the time was that by far the most popular band at these Friday night village dances was Jimmy Shand and his Band. Jimmy played nothing but Scottish music for Scottish dancing – arms aloft and kilts swirling! We gigged with Jimmy at Lockerbie Town Hall and opened the evening with all the current charts stuff from Beatles, Hollies, Searchers etc. We went down quite well and the floor was respectably full of teenagers. We played our first set and on came Jimmy and his band. In an instant the floor was full to the brim with three hundred people of all ages swirling and curling to the Gay Gordons and other Scottish eights and fours. We were absolutely stunned and had never seen anything like this since Joe Loss played Crewe Town Hall. The crowd was ecstatic and Jimmy carried the night with 'The Crescents frae Crewe' firmly in second spot. But you learn something with every new gig. That night it was that when two bands gig together it should not be a battle of the bands but a night in which both or all bands do their best to entertain the audience as well as you can with their own type of music and talent. That way you hopefully please the crowd and make good friends with the other performers. One of my proudest moments was having a pint of heavy and a good chat with Jimmy Shand!

Chapter Nine

November 22nd 1963

As you will no doubt know this date is indelibly burned into the memory of each and every one of us who is old enough to remember the early sixties. It was a Friday and we had a gig at the Horns Hotel in Wrexham. We had gigged there a few times previously and got on well with the landlady and her son, Tony, who worked at what was then known as Ringway Airport, now the very busy Manchester Airport. The Horns was a small pub surrounded by houses in the old part of Wrexham and always had a good atmosphere and a good sound due to a small room with a low ceiling. We would usually get there early and do a bit of rehearsing of new numbers using Tony as a soundboard audience. He was quite astute businesswise and had a good ear for what would be suitable or not for our repertoire.

Anyway the Friday lunchtime came and off we set having picked Dave up from Middlewich which was about eight miles from Crewe in the wrong direction. Bowling along quite merrily we were discussing what to do with our rehearsal time when our singing was supplemented by a loud and strange whining noise. Now I know what you are thinking, but no, it was not my singing, but a rather unmelodic bass part from our trusty old J2 van. Roger, who was the mechanic of the band, listened and pronounced the noise to be funny. Not funny ha ha, but funny peculiar. As our singing decreased in volume the van's offering increased alarmingly until it could have rivalled the decibels of a heavy metal band. 'Summat's up' was Roger's professional opinion. 'Aye. Tis' was the three voiced reply. The poor old van would go no more, at least on that day. What to do? The only thing open to us was to go to the pub! Ah, real Crewe guys I hear you say. In fact the nearest pub was the Red Lion right opposite the old Barony Hospital in Nantwich, so we decided to trek down there to ring Tony at the Horns. For those of you with the latest Apple iPhone, or Samsung Galaxy Nine, I must remind you that the year was 1963 and even Bill Gates was about eight years old at the time. There were still many years before any sort of mobile device was thought of, and not a great many houses had even a landline telephone. So we got to the pub and eventually got through to Tony. 'Sorry Tony, van problems, can't make it.'

'Don't worry, gigs off,' came the reply. 'Aren't you watching on the tele?' It was only then that we noticed that everyone in the pub was totally silent and were all watching intently as the TV anchor man was describing events in Dallas, Texas. It didn't take us long to realise that something was very wrong and probably the biggest story of the decade or even the century was unfolding before our eyes. Poor old John Kennedy had breathed his last and the world seemed changed forever. Everybody was extremely upset to say the least and some folks in the pub were in tears at the sight of the chaos and turmoil that was happening both in Dallas and indeed the whole of the western world. We stayed in the Red Lion till about nine pm watching and listening to various experts giving their thoughts on who was responsible for the outrage, then eventually we rang a friend to come and pick us up to trek back home. Next day the van was fixed and we were ready to go on our way earning our living and doing our best, but as everyone who lived through that time will tell you, things changed from then on and there was a sadness and melancholy through our world that took a long time to fade. But life goes on and stories become history as new horizons open and new paths are taken.

Chapter Ten

The Night We Nearly Burned Loch Lomond

We had been booked to play a Sunday night gig at the big hotel on the lochside at Balloch, which was a very pleasant small town on the south side of Loch Lomond. We were the support band to The Tremoloes who had by then left Brian Poole and gone on their own and had quite a few chart successes. In fact I think it was the first night that Chip Hawkes, father of Chesney, played with the Tremoloes. They were very good indeed and sang their harmonies very tightly, and nice guys to chat with in a very big shared dressing room.

Earlier in the day we had booked into a B&B with an old lady who had two rooms to let in her bungalow which was not far up the shore of the lake from the hotel. After the gig and loading up we arrived at the bungalow about twelve thirty in the morning and used our key that we had been given earlier. The lady was probably well and truly asleep by this time. We had a quick wash and into bed, thoroughly shattered after the drive up from South England. It was a bitterly cold winter and we tried to find some sort of heater, but apart from trying some switches nothing appeared to come on to heat the room. I was in with Bernard and Dave and Roger shared the other room. About an hour later I woke up to smell some sort of burning. 'Bernie, Bernie, can you smell smoke?' 'No I don't think so,' but Bernie was a heavy smoker and his nose was probably bunged up with nicotine. 'Go back to sleep,' he grunted and turned over. Half an hour later.

'Bernie, Bernie, I can still smell smoke.' At this point I decided to go and tell the other two that we had told the old lady we would not smoke in the rooms. Next door all was silent except for two snoring rock and rollers. I came back to our room and decided to investigate as the smell was getting worse. I looked around and decided to pull out the wardrobe. Why I do not know, but if I hadn't pulled it out I don't think we or the old lady would have seen the light of day again. The whole of the back of the wardrobe was a charred mass of smouldering wood, with a fiery red rim that was just about to burst into flame.

'BERNIE, BERNIE, get some water.' Luckily there was a wash basin in the room and we filled some teacups and doused the wood until it resembled the smoking aftermath of a forest fire! What had happened was that one of the switches that we had tried was for a two barred, wall mounted electric fire, and the wardrobe had been placed right in front of the fire about two inches from the wood. We had switched on the fire without realising what we had done and the fire had happily done its job only too well. Eventually we got the wood cool and tried to clean it up as best we could. We slept with all the windows open and nearly froze to death during a night of minus seven degrees. Next morning the wardrobe was back in position, the room looked and smelled reasonably correct and we ate our breakfast and got out as quickly as we could. I often wonder whether our escapade was discovered or if the burned wardrobe is still there to this day. It is often said that Robert the Bruce saved Scotland at Bannockburn, but we like to think we also played a small part in stopping Ballochburn!

Chapter Eleven

The Darville Years

Round about the late autumn of 1963 we entered a talent competition for bands held at the Blue Ball Hotel in Prescott Street, Liverpool. We were very much out-of-towners with all the other twenty or so bands coming from the fair city. By that time we had realised that we all played at least two instruments and thus should make use of this and feature it in our show. We worked on a sequence we called 'The Rave' which consisted of the following - we started with something like Peggy Sue with me singing and Dave on bass, then Dave would go on to his keyboard and I would play bass. Roger would then do a drum solo which I would join in with to do a drum duet, and eventually take over on drums without a musical break in the rhythm. After this Roger would get on his tenor sax and we would all lead into The Can Can with a strong modern rock beat. All the other three would dance a bit of Can Can as a gimmick and we would develop into a big grand finish for the set. This went amazingly well in clubs and pubs and got us a lot of extra work as it was quite unusual at the time for every one of the band to double up on other instruments. We did this at the Blue Ball and the crowd went wild for us with a real Liverpool ovation. Before the semi-final of the competition we all went for a Chinese meal just across from the pub, where I remember having prawns and rice and eating quite a lot. We went back and did the first set in the pub and retired to the dressing room at the back of the stage. Pretty soon I felt very strange and almost immediately the prawns and rice did a re-appearing act all over the floor of the dressing room and eventually in the sink!! Not a pleasant situation I assure you. Brenda, Bernie's wife was tremendous in looking after yours truly and got me into a state where I could at least go up to receive the news that we had won the semi-final. Needless to say I did not take part in the second set. The funny thing was everybody thought I was absolutely ratted from the visit to the pub!!! Not true dear reader I assure you. We eventually won the whole thing in late November. To beat many other local bands as 'foreigners' was quite an achievement and we were well pleased that all our hard work was showing signs of success.

The competition was being judged by about five people, two of whom were Ken and Frances Smith who ran Darville Entertainments on Merseyside and KDS Agency in Birmingham. They approached us with a view to signing with them and we said we would think about it. At the same time we had worked for a Liverpool guy called Jim Turner who managed some of the well-known bands. He promised us a tour with Frankie Valli and the Four Seasons if we signed with him. After days of arguments and discussion we eventually signed with Ken Smith. Later on we found out that the Four Seasons tour was cancelled with the Musicians Union dispute so perhaps all was for the best. So what next? New manager, new territory, new stage clothes, new gigs. Where would it all lead???

Kenneth Darville Smith was from Birmingham and had run an agency down there called KDS. Ken and his wife Frances saw what was happening with the Merseybeat sound and upped sticks and moved to Thornton Hough, a rather posh village on the Wirral peninsular, just across the Mersey from what was rapidly becoming the world centre of popular music. Brian Epstein had the Beatles. Les Ackerley had the Searchers. Ted Knibbs had Billy J Kramer. Jim Ireland had the Swinging Blue Jeans and the list went on and on. The Liverpool venues that suddenly became famous were The Cavern, The Iron Door, The Peppermint Lounge, Litherland Town Hall, The Grafton Rooms, New Brighton Tower Ballroom and many more. It was summed up by the band list for St Thomas's Youth Club in Ellesmere Port on the Wirral. We played there in 1963 and looked at the bands advertised for previous gigs. The list today would cost over millions of pounds to put on. Bands included the Beatles, Gerry and the Pacemakers, The Fourmost, Freddie Starr and the Midnighters, Billy Kramer (as was), Rory Storm, The Bluejeans, The Searchers etc etc. This was a youth club with a capacity of about one hundred and twenty which was run by the priest from the adjoining church who was a really nice fella.

Things were developing elsewhere as well. If you can do it, use the internet to search on Wednesbury Youth Centre which was a Birmingham suburban youth club in the early to mid-sixties. You will be surprised by the band list. All the up and coming famous bands gigged there, but being in the Midlands they also had The Move, The Moody Blues, Ozzy Osbourne and others. Once again here we were looking at a fee of about £25 for the night. Most of the aforementioned would be on that sort of money originally before prices began to rocket. Ken Smith's proudest possession was a framed contract on his office wall for Maney Hall in Sutton Coldfield for the Beatles for £30 in 1962.

By now Phil Ryan and the Crescents were starting to travel further afield. With Ken's midlands contacts, as well as his Mersey office, gigs were more plentiful and further afield. When we were down in Birmingham we used to stay in a B&B with a lovely old lady named Mrs Reece. If I remember correctly it was in Sutton New Road in Erdington near a big pub called The Yenton. Possibly the pub and the road have long since disappeared, such is progress. Mrs Reece looked after us well over the years we stayed there but there was only one trouble. Her Brummie accent was so strong that none of us could understand what she said. However we all got on famously and had many a cup of tea and chat with this lovely lady. One of the nearby gigs was a club above a row of shops in Erdington. I think it was called the Carlton but could be wrong. It comes to mind as it appears in quite a few bands memoirs and internet pages about the good old days. Like the old Merseyside venues this club had hosted all the top Birmingham bands including names like Wood, Bonham, Osbourne, Lynne, Laine, Wayne, Powell and many others.

Going to one of the gigs in Birmingham we experienced a strange and different Midlands welcome from the driver of a car on the ring road. We had an old J2 BMC van which was a great servant over the years. It originally had 'Buxted Chickens' written all over the sides as they were the previous owners. We changed that to Phil Ryan and the Crescents, having been threatened with court action by Buxted who perhaps didn't want their name associated with a load of scruffy looking young musicians! Anyway, there we were in heavy traffic on the very busy ring road when seemingly we got involved in a race with a guy in a sporty dark blue car. We were just trying to get to Stirchley for a gig but he wanted to show the world that Stirling Moss was alive and well in Birmingham. I was driving the old J2 and like most people I don't like being cut up on the road by over ambitious prats!! The situation progressed with each of us overtaking each other with inches to spare when all traffic came to a halt. The guy got out of his car on the inside of us and motioned to Dave, who was in the passenger seat, to wind the window down. Dave did so and was the immediate recipient of a swift and full blooded right hook through the open window. The guy then sprinted off back to his car and took off like a bomb. The old J2 and I followed like mad after this fool to try and show him some Crewe justice. I nearly rammed about five cars trying to catch him but to no avail. Dave was left with a fat lip for the gig and the rest of us were seething and smarting. Still, you can't win 'em all can you? Try singing the top harmony to Barbara Ann with a fat lip! Not easy!

Walsall and Wolverhampton were other favourite spots for pub and club gigs at that time. The Three Men in a Boat was a great pub gig but at times a little rough and ready shall we say. Roger had his work cut out one night to stop a member of the audience from pouring his pint down the bell of his tenor sax. We weren't that bad, it's just that the beer always flowed copiously in Walsall! We made great friends with all the folks at the MEB club (Electricity Board) in Walsall and played there many, many times. Malcolm Mellors was the young secretary's name and his good friends Fred and Mary used to travel all over the area to come and see us at other gigs. Come to think of it we met some really great and pleasant people during our time on the road, friendly and generous was the norm with the younger ones.

A gig at The Yungfrau Club in Manchester. Gigs were getting better and further afield.

Some of the older generation of club owners were more often money minded. On the way to play at Swindon Locarno Roger, the drummer and sax player, suddenly felt ill and was not too good at all. What do you do in a van full of equipment and young guys on the A38 just South of Birmingham? We carried on as best we could but Roger became worse. One thing for it – hospital! By then we were nearly in Swindon so off we went to the local Emergency Unit. Roger was seen and kept in overnight as a precaution against worsening.

So!!! There we were. In the words of the book 'and then there were three.' We eventually found the Locarno where we were on with the Downliners Sect from London as equal top of the bill. The owner was a quaint old guy called Peter Reddaway, helped by his son Max. We did the gig with me playing drums all the way through. Thank God for the Hot Rod experience. We did as well as we could but as I was the lead singer I think my performance was somewhat limited. However we got through the gig and made a reasonable job of it. As we were packing down along came Peter with some money. 'Well lads, well done without your drummer,' he said with a smile. 'As I contracted for a four piece group and you were only three I have deducted £10 from the fee.' He then gave us £20 for the gig. We were just thankful to have got through the night and nobody had the heart to argue for any extra. We then zapped back to the hospital and found that Roger was fit to come back with us to Crewe having had some sort of mini collapse of his system as the doctor put it. It was no great surprise as in those days we were doing six nights a week, travelling about one thousand miles per week, eating egg and chips in transport cafes, and getting home at three o'clock most mornings. Not the healthiest of life styles.

We had a phone call from Ken Smith one day who seemed very excited about something. He'd been telephoned by a certain Mr Brian Epstein asking if The Crescents were able to provide backing music for one of his artists on a short tour of the south west. He set up a rehearsal at the OPB (Orrell Park Ballroom) on the A59 and we rolled up early in the morning to be greeted by none other than Cilla Black and husband to be Bobby. She had just had a top forty hit with 'Love of the Loved' and was obviously going to be a big star in the business. We all got on really well and I was impressed at what an ordinary, humorous young girl she was. Her voice was really fantastic with a deep rich style which retained its raw newness combined with a mature deep quality in tone. We kept stopping rehearsal for a brew and a butty and eventually got her set just right for the city of Bath, where we were going to work for an agent called Bud Godfrey, based in the Regency ballroom in Bath city itself. Cilla had by that time recently recorded 'Anyone who had a Heart' but couldn't remember the words or the tune as she had never done it in public. Strange! I hear you say. However this is true. I can vouch for the fact that when you record a song for any purpose if you don't immediately put it in your act you will forget it. I have done this myself and been quite embarrassed on stage!

CILLA BLACK

Britain's bright new beat songstress
—— the gal with the jet black voice

Sole Management/Direction : NEMS ENTERPRISES LTD.,
24 MOORFIELDS, LIVERPOOL 2

CILLA BLACK
recording for the Parlophone label

Probably one of the few pre-nose job photos of Cilla, 1964,
a lovely lady with a great voice.

The week came and went without any problem and the band once again was carried through by the musicianship of Bernard and Roger, with Dave filling in well on bass. On stage Cilla was terrific with a great scouse humour and a natural ability to work an audience. The crowd loved her and also Phil Ryan and the Crescents, as we went through the night as smoothly as possible. She did nearly an hour's spot and left the whole ballroom in a state of happy appreciation at being in the forefront of welcoming a new megastar to the pop scene.

Cilla left me a nice message and photo which is here in the book. A little later on we had a gig in Bristol with Unit 4-plus 2 at the Pavilion. We did the gig on a Tuesday, I think, but arrived to repeat on the Friday to find the ballroom and the park under about two feet of water from the river. No gig – no money – damn!!

Chapter Twelve

Abbey Road

By now thoughts had turned to recording. If all the other bands we worked with had had hit records, why shouldn't we?! We turned over lots of ideas and were given demos to listen to by Ken. However we all agreed that the song that was the most commercial was a version of an old spiritual folk song called 'Mary don't you Weep'. I'd learned this at school in Stoke when messing about with some guitar mates during opera rehearsals in the Christmas holiday of 1960. I'd put in a few different chord changes to make it sound more modern and possibly a bit cleverer.

Early in 1964 off we went to Northampton Sound Services to create a demo of 'Mary'. The studio and staff there were really professional and friendly and in half a day we had a very creditable piece of vinyl to take back home. It's surprising what studio work does for your performance. On the road at normal gigs, whether big or small, you can make mistakes and they don't really matter as they pass over quickly and the audience don't hinge on the mistake but just carry on listening to your performance. In the studio things are vastly different.

Even the tiniest error shows up like the proverbial sore thumb. You really have to concentrate like mad to achieve anything like a quality effort. I have heard professional sportsmen saying that they lost concentration for half a minute and the opposition scored. I now knew exactly how they felt. We had to keep our minds so focussed on the playing and singing that at the end of the session we were all well and truly knackered! This is a technical musical term! However all went well and Ken listened and agreed with us that it was pretty good. He was in the know about agents and managers and sent it to EMI where the chief A&R man was Norrie Paramour. Now Norrie was a really big wheel in the music business both for EMI and all the television and radio companies. Every week you would see his smiling face leading orchestras on all the big TV shows. He must have liked what he heard because he invited us down to Abbey Road to do a recording test for possible release. Abbey Road!!! Wow. We were on cloud nine. If nothing ever came of it we were going to Abbey Road – zebra crossing and all!! In those days bands did a record test to see if they were good enough to have a recording contract. Later on came the idea that you bought studio time anywhere, produced your own record and tried to sell it to the big companies like Decca, EMI or Polydor for them to release. We had done it the hard way, but for us this was fine as EMI paid for everything from studio time to publicity and promotional work.

Normal bands got three hours of studio time and the bigger bands got to choose their time of day. Most of the stars chose late evening as by then the voice has had time to warm up well over the day and the body is in fine form to work. You will have heard of the Beatles and Stones working through the night to complete successful discs. You can guess what our studio time was - nine o'clock in the morning till midday. At that time hotels in London were not cheap so we set off from Crewe about five in the morning to be sure of arriving in time. At the appointed time we were there, bleary eyed, coughing and spluttering and knackered – but we were there - Abbey Road, St John's Wood. London. We were put in studio 3 to record Mary and began to set up our instruments etc. It was quite scary being somewhere that had seen the greatest of stars and musicians under its roof. Our A&R man was a young man called Bob Barratt who was a really great young guy with a cut glass public school accent. He made us feel very welcome and at home and we started to work. In only a few takes 'Mary' was done. It turned out well and we all had crossed fingers for the result. Bernard and Dave had been writing a few songs and one of theirs, 'Yes I Will' was chosen by Bob for the B Side of a possible release. To this day some folks still say that EMI got the A and B sides the wrong way around and the B side was more commercial. Anyway twelve o'clock came and off we trekked back up north. Things must have been good because in no time came news that Norrie was pleased with the outcome and wanted to put his string section on Mary. A contract was on its way in the post for release later in 1964. We were in! A recording group for Ken Smith, Crewe's first recording group. Better gigs, better money, stardom on its way!

Chapter Thirteen

The First Hamburg Trip

As it was the summer of 1964 work in UK tailed off a bit and things were a bit slow on the financial side. What to do? Well when you don't have a lot of the old loot chinking in your pocket do as all the other Liverpool bands had been doing for years. Go to Germany. We looked at various deals for various agents and although the work was hard the money was quite good. As mentioned earlier on in the book most deals were paying twenty five pounds per man per week with accommodation and some food thrown in. If you played in a club serving food you could always get a free plateful at some time be it seven at night or four in the morning! We chatted with Ken and eventually he set us up in a deal with Manfred Woitala to do the months of September and October. Now Manfred was a youngish businessman who knew the ropes backwards and was extremely cute in his deals, but we found him OK to work for as we worked hard for him and he appreciated that. It wasn't till years later that we discovered that old Manfred had connections to what I will call the seedier and greyer part of Hamburg nightlife. I suppose that like most night clubs and drinking clubs anywhere, people of the underworld are attracted by the lifestyle and late night gambling that goes on.

Roger, Dave and Bernard along with Terry, Kevin, Allan and Jake from the Delmonts, waiting to board the ferry to the Hook of Holland, 31 August 1964 – my twenty first birthday!

Anyway our contract was to start on September 1st and we had to be there and ready to play on the day at the appointed hour. We booked our travel from Harwich to the Hook of Holland for the 31st of August which was my twenty first birthday. I think my Mum and Dad were disappointed that son number two was going to be somewhere in the middle of the North Sea rather than having a big family party to celebrate having the key of the door. However work is work, so off we went.

We had a gig at Lysaght's Steelworks in Scunthorpe on the night of Sunday 30 August which was on the way to Harwich. We did the gig well and the cash payment helped with travelling costs for the next twenty four hours. Now in a sixties band you saved money wherever possible, so we did what every band in history, even superstars, will have done at some time in the past. We slept in the van in a layby halfway down the A15. Next morning bright and early, about 5 o'clock, we were awoken by the noise of big ten wheelers thrashing past at sixty miles an hour, off to wherever their load was destined. With throats like sandpaper and looking a little worse for wear, off we went in search of the docks and the continent of Europe.

We arrived to find our travelling companions already there having driven down from Liverpool that morning. Ken worked with lots of bands and he had booked us to travel along with the Delmont Four who we knew from the Blue Ball talent competition and got on very well with. Unknown to us they had been supplemented by a singer from Birkenhead who had left his own band and was off to Germany to try his luck using the Delmonts as his backing group. His name was Freddie Starr! Now Freddie was a piece of work. I believe that is the best way to describe him. It will suffice to say that he was, and probably still is, a one off character. He is a small guy with a huge presence, made larger by his unquenchable thirst for gags, humour and stories. As a singer Freddie was OK, like a lot of other singers at the time, but as a worker of an audience I had rarely seen anyone as good and as sharp as him. His timing was brilliant and his reaction to a live crowd was second to none.

Our boat sailed on the early tide of my birthday and we all tried to get some sleep on chairs dotted around the lounge. I used to have a lovely picture of our van twenty five feet in the air being hoisted onto the boat in a sort of rope sling. It was the thing those days to lift vans onto the boat rather than the later roll-on roll-off type of ferry. Just as I was dozing off came the first of quite a few announcements asking for Mr Philip Rylance to go to the purser's office as soon as possible.

Now what, I thought, as I nervously found the purser who met me with a big grin and said 'Happy Birthday Sir on your 21st,' and gave me a telegram from Mum and Dad who wished me a happy birthday and said they were very proud of me! Believe it or not that brought the odd tear to my eyes. I ask you a tough, hard Liverpool based Rock'n'Roll singer in tears on a ferry boat? Never – well not often. With the telegram tucked in my back pocket I returned to my almost comfortable chair to try and resume my rest. This was not to be, as during the next half an hour the same thing happened three more times with three more announcements and three more telegrams, one from

Ken and Frances, the Darville management team, one from the wives and girlfriends of the other guys in the band and one from my uncles and aunts. Eventually the captain of the ferry came on the tannoy system and told the whole of the boat, passengers and crew that today was the 21st birthday of one of his passengers, Phil Rylance, who was a singer off to play in Germany with a Liverpool band. Fame at last before we'd even played a note!

The Hook of Holland eventually arrived and we started across Europe to our German destination sometime around late afternoon. In those far off days even in mainland Europe good motorway type roads were few and far between, especially round cities, so progress was slow around The Hague, Rotterdam and other Dutch conurbations. Eventually we hit good roads and drove north east towards Bremen and Hamburg on the famous German autobahns. Traffic flow was good and we made good progress into a long night's drive. I had driven earlier in the day so Bernard and Roger were taking it in turns as Dave and I slept in the back of the van. We weren't carrying much equipment as the German gigs and clubs always provided their own amps and PA systems. Great, good quality stuff was provided such as Gibson and Fender amps and Bayer microphone systems. All we had to bring was drums and guitars which left lots of room for things like sleep and space!

Eventually our two intrepid drivers stopped for some food whilst the two sleepers carried on snoozing in the back. Bernard and Roger came back moaning and groaning because the transport café owner didn't quite understand egg and chips. He got the egg ok but the chips were a non - starter as far as sign language and gesticulation were concerned. Egg on toast ruled the day and the drivers remained chip-less. Undaunted we carried on regardless and made good progress for the next few hours. However good progress was not to be. As we happily bowled along singing our first set harmonies (we used to rehearse in our van on the way to gigs) we suddenly lost most of the BMC fifteen cwt of immense power and our faithful old J2 went putt, putt, putt and spluttered to a near halt. By some sort of extreme luck we were near an autobahn service station with a repair bay and managed to get to the pull-in nearby. Two young German mechanics came out and pushed the van into their little workshop. 'If they can't understand egg and chips, don't hold your breath,' was Dave's comment. However after about half an hour one of the guys came out with a smile on his face and said 'Die Schwimmer im der Vergaser ist kaput,' which using literal translation reads something like this - 'The thing that swims in the gas making machine is broken.' But if you translate it into mechanic's language it reads, 'The float in the carburettor is punctured.' Believe it or not after ten minutes and a little silver soldering of the offending float we were back on the road with the great German guys not accepting anything for their labours. How's that for good Anglo-German relations? Brilliant!

So off we went and reached our destination without further ado. Our first gig was in the Kohlmarkt in Braunschweig in Schleswig Holstein. This was the Cabbage Market in Brunswick. We were to spend three weeks here playing every night from about eight o'clock till one in the morning. Forty five minutes on –fifteen minutes off. Now we had never done anything like this before. Our usual gigs were two forty five minute spots in the Wagon and Horses in Meir, Stoke on Trent, or three twenty fives at the Valley Club in Rockwood Avenue,

Crewe. All of a sudden we were doing about four hours per night and working our tiny little socks off for our money. Playing like this does wonders for the quality of your performance and we soon became a better and tighter band than we had ever been before. The German audiences loved our swapping over of instruments and called it 'Mach Schau' and sometimes clapped and cheered for minutes on end, and best of all put beer after beer on the side of the stage. The big hits of the day were Wooly Bully from Sam the Sham and the Pharaohs and Mr Tambourine Man from The Byrds and we finished up playing these two songs about eight times a night. The strange thing is we never ever rehearsed Wooly Bully. It was such an easy song that we listened to it on a little radio, worked out the key and chords, wrote down the words and put it into our set that night.

During this three weeks we had free accommodation, and I use that term loosely! We were billeted in one medium sized room at the back of the club, near the toilets. There were four bunks and nothing else in the room except four chairs and a table. I think we had one shower in three weeks and that was at the local swimming baths! We would finish playing at one o'clock most nights and then go out for a drink at a local late bar, come back and play poker with the waiters at the club. Wolfgang and Kuddel were good guys and looked after us well and often we would finish cards at about four o'clock, have another drink at a bar and then crawl into bed about six or seven in the morning. We managed to turn night into day and slept, badly, between eight and two in the afternoon. When we woke we all wanted breakfast. At two in the afternoon! Just about the only place open at that time was the railway station just across the road, and we managed to practically live at the place with our favourite menu being Speigeleier mit Bratkartoffeln. With apologies to all good German speakers that is my translation of fried egg and chips - all for one and eight pence! The meal cost one Deutschmark and it was, in those days, twelve to the pound. Hope my maths is correct here. Beer and fags were very cheap so we were drinking a lot and I was practically chain smoking. Perhaps pneumonia in later life had something to do with that.

At this time I must mention that for A level history at school, my period to study was European History 1648 to 1815. Now that will ring a distinct bell with some readers. Here I was with a rock and roll band right in the middle of the city where the Elector of Brunswick reviewed his troops before the Seven Year's War. Here I was in 1964 sitting in the main square in this beautiful city and drinking in the atmosphere of the huge Platz, the cobbled streets and the balconies. If only St Joseph's College could have brought me here I might have passed!

The three weeks passed quite quickly and we were off to Hanover (not more A level!). This place was extremely badly damaged during the war and thus was mainly rebuilt with modern methods. It had the widest streets I had ever seen, with four traffic lanes each way on either side of tram/rail tracks down the middle. From the shop fronts on one side was about one hundred yards to the opposite shops. We did a week here in a very modern and posh night club with a roof which opened in fine night weather to reveal stars in the sky – very impressive. Accommodation was in a real hotel with B&B which suited us fine. As we did our first night's set we noticed that there were a lot of young English people in the audience. Upon chatting and asking a few questions we realised that all these folks were part of BAOR, British Army of the Rhine. For those of you old enough to remember Family Favourites you will recall Cliff Michelmore and Jean Metcalf on a Sunday morning reading out endless addresses from BFPO 40, 50, 47, 41, etc etc. Little did I then realise that many years later I would live at BFPO 40 in Moenchengladbach for twenty years!

The Hanover gig went well for seven nights and then off we went to Kiel right up on the Baltic coast. Now if you have gigged in Liverpool or other northern cities you will have seen life with a capital L. Kiel was something similar but in spades. Life was rough and tough in this cosmopolitan outpost. Sailors of every nationality were to be found twenty four hours a day on the lookout for somewhere to spend their cash. This attracted a large amount of what we shall call wheelers and dealers of both sexes! The Star Palast Club, our venue, was near the docks and was an old cinema or theatre where the waiters were also the bouncers, and all of them carried a night stick in their waistband and some carried guns!! I kid you not! We did a week here with a band from Chippenham called Steve Law and the Group Four. We all got on well and had many happy hours spinning yarns and drinking in the club after all the customers had gone home – about half past five in the morning! On quite a few occasions we witnessed a disturbance in the club with drunken sailors prepared to let their fists do the talking for them. It was at these times we realised that the waiters were not to be argued with – under any circumstances at all.

The Kiel week went down well and the young German people seemed to be well in tune with our kind of music, with a lot of harmony, Beatles and a bit of good old fashioned Rock'n'Roll.

It was time to move to Eckernforde about fifty miles up the coast on the way to Denmark. This was where the infamous Unter Wasser Waffen Schule was during the war. The Undersea Warfare Training School was where U-Boat crews were trained before setting out on their missions to attack allied shipping. We saw nothing of the place and didn't even know whether it still existed at the time. The club we were to work at was The Star Palast again, situated in an old cinema, near the Baltic Sea. It all sounds very cold but actually the weather for early October was quite warm and pleasant and we were able to amble along the sandy beach whenever we had the time during the afternoon. The playing hours were much the same as all the other gigs with Saturday being a long session and Sunday starting at four pm and finishing about midnight. However each weekend day there were at least two bands if not more, so we did get some good breaks.

The following weeks were in Bucholz and Luneburg. In the Bucholz club we were sleeping in the projection room of the old cinema which was not the best arrangement as there were still pigeon holes for the film projectors to shine through the walls of the room. These holes led to the main hall and so there was always the echo and the noise of the sea, amongst other things, in the bedroom. The playing once again was good and we managed to learn more songs on the hoof, as it were, without much rehearsal. Skinny Minnie, the old Bill Haley classic, was requested one night by a rather drunken Norwegian sailor. 'Right,' said Bernard, 'in G,' and off we went playing the aforementioned in the key of G. It went so well that it stayed in our repertoire until the end of the band in 1966!

The town of Luneburg was a beautiful small village type of place about one hundred miles south of the coast on the other side of Hamburg. The main square had the most fabulous black and white buildings about five stories high which reminded us very much of Nantwich or Chester from back home. It was hunting, shooting and fishing territory and every shop seemed to sell equipment for these pastimes. I remember buying a very sharp flick knife with a bone antler handle as a sort of memento of the town and the area. The upshot of this was that a very inexperienced young singer declared it to customs on the return to England and watched as a very serious officer threw it in a security bin and made me sign the dangerous imported implements register. Ah well!

Once again the club was a Star Palast, but this one was managed by Karl-Heinz who was Manfred Woitala's brother in law. Now Karl–Heinz liked his German beer, as did Phil Ryan and the Crescents, so as each evening progressed, if we were going down well, copious amounts of very tasty Luneburger Pils found their way to the stage. In fact on quite a few of the week's nights the old band had a few problems with walking straight. Not to worry though as we were sleeping directly opposite the club door in a small hotel. So the routine became sleep, eat, drink, play, drink, eat, drink, play, sleep, sleep, but not necessarily in that order! Eventually our German work came to an end and with quite a bit of sadness, but with great expectations, we set off across the German plains back to The Hook and England. Back to what we hoped would be a hit record for Christmas 1964.

Chapter Fourteen

Mary Don't You Weep

After sleeping for what seemed like a week in a comfy bed we were ready to prepare ourselves for a major assault on the record industry. EMI had been in touch and sent us a pre-release copy of 'Mary' and we all gathered, parents and all, at Ken's bungalow in Thornton Hough. The drinks were served and we all sat round expectantly for our very first listen. The opening bars were as we recorded them, but when we got to the second verse Norrie's orchestra faded in with some very commercial violin riffs and more augmented parts. We were absolutely thrilled as our eyes opened wide and grins as big as yer face appeared. Everyone in the room agreed that the sound was very commercial and had great possibilities for the charts. The journey back to Crewe was spent discussing the plans to go forward from here. We appointed a publicity agent from Chester named Keith Gronbach, who was going to cost us £40 per month, which we considered reasonable as long as he did his job well. The date EMI had given us for release was Friday, November 20th 1964.

Our various factions swung into action and all systems were go to set up a campaign of publicity to try and grab the media, both local and national. It's very interesting to see how things work in this type of business and we were all quite naïve in the workings of the media machine. Whilst we carried on earning our living by the usual run of the mill gigs, Ken and Keith were busy planning a blockbuster release day extravaganza!

Surrounded by fans, Phil Ryan and the Crescents, pictured with Crewe's Stationmaster.

Both pics from The Crewe Chronicle

THEIR FIRST RECORD A HIT

Phil Ryan (second, left) with the Crescents, left to right Roger Knay, David Birkenhead and Bernard Hibbert, busy signing record covers at Breeden and Middleton's

WITHIN an hour of Phil Ryan and the Crescents' first record, "Mary Don't You

The recording—and the reverse side "Yes I will"—was relayed over Breeden and Middleton's reception loudspeaker equipment.

Among those waiting at the station were the two oldest members of the group's fan club Mr. and Mrs. Thomas Lancaster, from Blackpool. Mr. Lancaster is 73

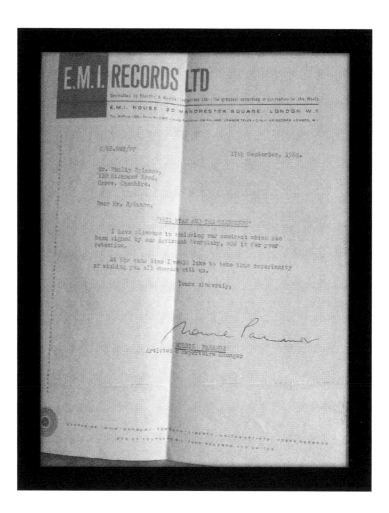

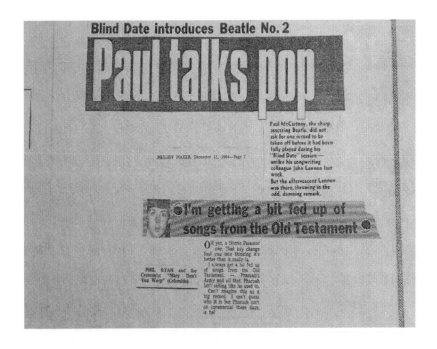

Paul McCartney reviewed our first EMI effort for the Melody Maker magazine. As you can see he was not over impressed. Ah well! Back to the drawing board. The Melody Maker was the trade paper to read in those days. It held terrific sway with musicians from all genres. Perhaps it's Paul's fault we didn't get to number one!!

Eventually the big day arrived and we set off to Sandbach, six miles away, to get on the Scotland to London train. Why, I hear you ask. The idea was that the public would be told we were returning from a Scottish tour to our hometown for the release of our chartbusting hit! Our loyal fans were to be swarming around the platform awaiting the return of their heroes from far off lands. Well the train was late, as ever, and eventually we arrived in Crewe Station to be met and welcomed by the station master, Kenneth Winterton, in his top hat outfit surrounded by our banner waving crowd. It all passed off very well and we were interviewed by local press etc and whisked off to the Odeon cinema to do a live appearance at the Saturday Morning Club. Little did we know it but Keith had tipped off the press about out non -existent Scottish tour and we were exposed in the News of the World on the following Sunday. It didn't seem to matter one bit and as Keith told us, 'There is no such thing as bad publicity.'

From the Odeon we were whisked off to Breedon and Middletons, the local large record store, to be met by 'Mary Don't you Weep' being blasted from all parts of the shop. Our fan club was being run by Shirley and Elaine from Timperley and they had circulated details of this event to all members and thus we had a happy throng and sat for about an hour signing record sleeves. The evening came and Ken had booked us into the Civic Hall in Nantwich as top of the bill. He was promoting the dances at the Civic so that was no problem at all and the gig went really well. We had a bit of a hero's welcome and eventually all four of us went home absolutely exhausted. Being a star is very tiring!!!
We watched the charts over the next week and were amazed that we were not number one. However Mary sold seven thousand in the first week of sales and after a very short time we had a letter from EMI Columbia and Norrie Paramour offering us a contract for another two releases in 1965.
Wow!!! Great stuff. However the hoped for number one slot

did not materialise, but eventually we did make the charts at number 39 in the top 40 for one week.

Crewe's Mayor is one of their fans

WHEN a Crewe beat group, Phil Ryan and the Crescents, heard that the Mayor of Crewe, Mrs. Nellie V. Patrick, was one of their fans, they decided to make her an honorary member of their Fan Club and present her with a copy of their latest record, "Gypsy Woman," which is to be released tomorrow (Friday).

So the Mayor arranged an official reception in the Mayor's Parlour, and our picture shows Mrs. Patrick inspecting the new disc with Phil

(seated) and the Crescents (left to right): Roger Keay, David Birkenhead and Bernard Hibbert.

The group will sing their record and be interviewed by Muriel Young on the Radio Luxembourg show, "Friday Spectacular," on June 4.

Crescents cut first disc

Liverpool began it in 1963; Manchester carried on in 1964; and now the latest town to join the North's take-over of pop music is Crewe.

Phil Ryan and the Crescents have made their disc debut with "Mary Don't You Weep" a traditional biblical ditty which Phil (front centre) arranged to fit the current trend.

Lead guitarist Bernard Hibbert (top) and David Birkenhead (right) on bass, combined to write "Yes I Will" the B side of what could well become a hit.

Bernard, 21, was a clerk in the works accountant's office. Drummer Roger Keay, also 21, was a clerk in the loco stores, and 19-year-old David, from Middlewich, also had a rail job.

In their home town the new record was sold out in the first few days of release, and with several spins on radio programmes, the Crewe Sound may soon mean something more than the "works buzzer." — PETER KENT.

As part of the promotional stuff for EMI groups there were always Radio Luxembourg shows to do to help push the name around the pop business. In our ignorance we imagined jetting off to the Grand Duchy to be interviewed by a well-known DJ. In fact our Grand Duchy was situated in the basement studio of the EMI headquarters in Manchester Square, Soho. This was the same building that featured in the scene of the Beatles looking over the rail on the cover of the Please Please Me albums. On the appointed day of recording we trogged off to London and after a slow and traffic laden journey we arrived and were met by Shaw Taylor, who at that time was a Luxembourg DJ of some renown. We all got on well and he ran through a bit of a rehearsal to try and make things a bit light hearted. The plan was to do something like this.

Shaw - Hi Phil. Did you have a good journey down today from the North?

Phil - Hi Shaw. Unfortunately we had a breakdown.

Shaw – Oh dear, not a nervous one I hope.

(Pause for audience laughter).

Now we were all knackered, a bit nervous and a bit in awe of the situation of being on Radio Lux. So this how it actually went.

Shaw – Hi Phil. Did you have a good journey down today from the North?

Phil – Hi Shaw. Unfortunately we had a crash.

There was a few seconds pause as Shaw looked at me, I looked at him and he must have thought to himself 'What a right one we have here.' He looked around and tried his best with, 'Oh no, not a sort of nervous crash or breakdown eh?'

We never heard Shaw Taylor on Luxembourg ever again, but eventually he emerged as the host of Police 5 and did very well too.

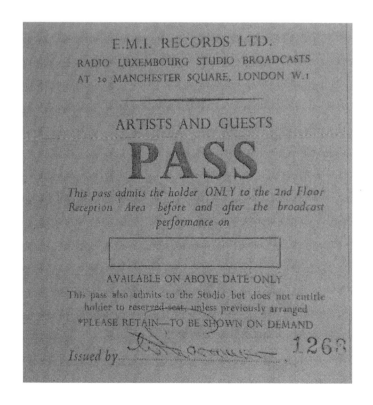

Chapter Fifteen

Back to Normality

After all the excitement of release day, Luxembourg, local interviews and even a Melody Maker review by Paul McCartney things quietened down and we went back to normal gigs. Money did increase as a result of Mary and we even got up to £75 for a New Year's Eve gig at the Plaza in Handsworth, where we actually topped the bill to Roy Wood's band, Mike Sheridan and the Night Riders. Trouble was, they were a lot better than we were. Ah well - such is life!

The new year of 1965 came along quickly and we plunged into gigs hoping to make a success in the aftermath of an Abbey Road release. Snow came and went and the Crescents rolled on towards the next EMI recording session. Bob Barratt had sent us a demo of a Curtis Mayfield song called Gypsy Woman which eventually became the next release and off we went to record. The same time of day was used for our session and we arrived bleary eyed and shattered in Abbey Road, studio two, at nine am prompt. However all went well and we finished both sides in our allotted three hours. As before Norrie decided to over - dub some bits, but this time didn't use the Norrie Paramour Strings but used a young up and coming guitarist by the name of Jeff Beck, or so the story goes. The finished article didn't sound too bad at all and we were all quite pleased that our second release was in the can, as they say. Gigs rolled on until the release date in early spring 1965. We went through the publicity rigmarole again with visits to London and Radio Luxembourg recordings in the EMI basement, no Shaw Taylor this time! Eventually release Friday came and we did a few more appearances and publicity things to help promote the record. Once again we had great hopes of some sort of minor chart success.

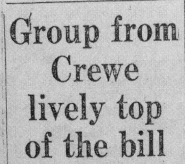

Group from Crewe lively top of the bill

A Cheshire group, Phil Ryan and the Crescents, from Crewe, topped the bill at the King's Hall, Stoke, on Saturday.

Phil and his group made their debut disc last year entitled "Mary Don't You Weep," but the record enjoyed only mild success.

The choice of material was very wide—from ballad to beat—and the group gave a very lively and confident performance, in keeping with their reputation.

Although the group have not made many appearances in the city, they proved popular with the dancers.

Another record

Phil told the *Sentinel* that he and the group would soon be making another record.

Also on the bill were Tony Gaelic and the Gaelics.

I think we had learned last time that this chart business was all connected to who you knew, how much money was behind you and whether your face fitted!

I don't think the money was there from Ken Smith as he was a rather small fish in a very large pond, which was controlled by the established forces of the industry. We got on OK with Norrie and Bob at EMI but that was the technical and artistic side of things. It didn't take us long to realise that the publicity and promotional side was far more important as far as record sales went. All record companies had record pluggers and sales boosters whose job was to contact all the important people in the TV and radio broadcasting business and get them to play and plug our record. As in any business there were always short cuts to success and a bonus to be earned which usually concerned the one factor that makes the world go round; money, money, money! Gypsy Woman had no real financial backing and after an initial week of about three thousand sales it all went very quiet.

Sometime later we were astonished to see headlines in the music press which read, 'Gypsy Woman tops US charts'. Wow, we thought with pictures of Cadillacs and swimming pools conjured up in our minds. Should we have a Hollywood mansion or would a New York apartment be better. We dashed to the newsagents, bought a copy of New Musical Express and eagerly turned to the charts page, and there it was. Top of the charts in the Billboard Hot One Hundred, Gypsy Woman. There was only one huge problem. The name on the number one record of the week was Major Lance, not Phil Ryan. Major deflation was the order of the day. Unknown to us,

Major Lance, who was a well-established artist in the USA, had released a version of our song and it had gone almost straight to number one! Ah well. There was always another chance with the contracted third release for later in the year.

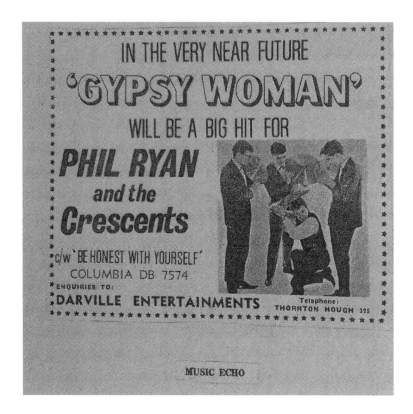

MUSIC ECHO

Normality continued with our regular haunts of the Scottish borders, Sheffield clubs, Birmingham dance halls and far flung one-off gigs all over UK. We met some great, friendly people on our travels and we always made sure that we were punctual, polite and pleasant wherever we went. One particular gig comes to mind. It was the Christmas day of one of our travelling years and we had a gig at Sheffield Lane Top, which was one of the most well-known of the city clubs. We were doing 'noon and neet' which meant you played over lunch time and then did the evening session. Whenever we did this we would go down to the Wicker in the city centre to a Chinese restaurant, I think called the Peacock. In our business Christmas day was like any other day. If there was a job to be had, you went and did it. Money was always good on festive days so off we had gone at nine o'clock over the Pennines to Sheffield. After we had finished our noon session to a packed house of what seemed like a men only session (in those days the wives and families came along on Sunday night if the band was any good at lunchtime), the steward and his wife said 'Where are you going for lunch lads?'

'Not sure, probably the Peacock,' was the reply.
'No you're not. You're eating here with us. Four o'clock, prompt!' Four o'clock arrived and we all sat down to the biggest turkey we had ever seen in our lives. Our Christmas dinner that year was one of the most memorable. There were these two kind and generous people who we had never ever met before inviting us into their home to share their Christmas dinner with them and their family. Happy days, good times and many, many friendly great people.

Chapter Sixteen

A Short Summer Season!

Summer loomed large in the distance and there was always an awkward lack of jobs unless you did a summer season. Ken Smith, in his wish to broaden his empire, decided to try and put together a summer tour for us and the Delmonts which included six nights per week in the southern half of England. Looking back now it was always going to be a non-starter as the mileage was huge and the pre-planning was not what it should have been on Ken's part. The venues were Brighton, Weston Super Mare, Felixstowe and one other which never ever materialised. If you put in a round tour map it looks bad enough for these three venues but they didn't roll off in one round trip.

For some reason Ken had booked Brighton for Monday, Weston for Tuesday, Brighton again for Wednesday and Felixstowe for Thursday. I ask you dear reader to please read that last sentence again, get out your RAC road map and look at the route and the timings. Well, after one week it was obvious that things would have to change. We played the Monday Brighton gig in a little dance club right on the seafront near the pier in a sort of walkway underpass. It was a nice venue, very smart and just the right thing for a sixties Mersey-Sound group. The only problem was the audience consisted of about seven people. Never mind. Wednesday will be better!

Off we went to Weston Super Mare to set up in a cafe which at night was transformed into a dance club for teenagers. Once again the same problem arose. There were not many teenagers wanting to be entertained by or dance to Phil Ryan and the Crescents and The Delmont Four, 'sparkling new bands from The Mersey' as the posters said. Back to Brighton then. The Wednesday gig turned out to be exactly the same, with an even smaller audience if that was at all possible. The playing was OK and we all had a bit of a laugh and giggle as bands do when they almost outnumber their audience.

So off we went to Felixstowe for the Thursday. Here we got a pleasant surprise and found about two hundred and fifty people at the evening venue which I think was the Floral Hall, possibly now the Spa Pavilion. Felixstowe was the only gig of our grand summer tour that survived. Ken quickly realised that to pay two bands, venue hire, advertising and promotional fees was going to cripple Darville Entertainments extremely quickly.

Brighton and Weston Super Mare were kicked into touch and the trip to deepest Suffolk became a weekly event for us every Thursday for the early part of the summer of 1965. From Crewe this was a long way but work was work and we made reasonable money for our long trek. This was of course before the advance of the motorway system and the only bits in existence was really part of the M1 and the Preston Bypass. We used to leave Crewe at nine in the morning, pass through Stoke on Trent, Market Harborough, Godmanchester, Cambridge, Bury St Edmunds and eventually arrive in Felixstowe about four o'clock in the afternoon. Each week there were different teenagers in the audience mostly holidaying with their parents, but including some local folks. It all went well and lasted until the end of Ken's contract on the venue when things new began to appear on the horizon. One incident that remains in the old grey matter from the whole tour is the first night of Weston Super Mare.

The Delmonts and the Crescents were due to sleep over in Weston before the long trek back to Brighton for the Wednesday as travelling in a J2 van in the early 60s was, to put it bluntly, knackering! We found a small hotel about midday of the very first Tuesday and both bands moved into their rooms to shower, kip and relax before the evening gig. Now The Delmonts were experienced travellers and had a distinct shortage of money as most of them had wives and young families back in Liverpool. At about six o'clock they packed all their stuff back in their van and went off to do the gig. Straight after the gig off they shot back up north to Liverpool without returning to the hotel leaving a very irate hotelier with used rooms, used shower and dirty bed linen. We returned to the hotel to be met with a form of Spanish inquisition from the owner as to the names, whereabouts and addresses of the Delmonts. We didn't exactly tell any lies but said that we couldn't help him very much as we didn't know where they lived, but we thought it was Liverpool. Anyway the hotel owner did no more than jump in his car and hare after them to try and remonstrate about their behaviour and demand payment for his room. It might be a good thing that he didn't find them as the four guys in the band had been Scouser born and bred and were extremely able to look after themselves in times of, shall we say, altercations!

Chapter Seventeen

Return to Germany

What next for a would-be-famous rock 'n roll band? Where else could a band go when there was little work in England, a summer season had backfired and a record had almost sunk without trace? Germany... yes indeed, Ken fixed us up with another two month tour using the same management and venues that we had used the previous year. Now this was fine for us as we had gone down well with the German crowds, money wasn't at all bad and we knew the score better than the year before. So off we trekked once more across the northern part of Europe to go straight to Kiel and the Star Palast for about three weeks. We had a good welcome from last year's friends, and the managers liked us as we brought in good crowds. We did the same venues as before and about half way through we did a week in Bucholz at the old cinema. Looking back now we experienced a situation which was to have a big effect on us and which completely knocked the stuffing out of four young intrepid musicians.

During the week we left most of the instruments on the stage after the night's playing and went upstairs to our bedroom in the projection room. This was done as we often used to rehearse during the day and found it easier to just walk on stage and start. However, we came down one day to find Bernard's guitar and a new Shure microphone missing from the stage. We presumed that the other band had moved it as they had been working earlier on in the day. No such luck. After much questioning and gesticulating we found the cleaner, who told us that the guitar repair man had been in to collect a guitar for repair and service!! The unfortunate truth was that there was no guitar repair man and no service for guitars. What had happened was that some chancer of a conman had walked in off the street, picked up Bernard's brand new Gibson SG and waltzed off into the morning sunshine with about four hundred pounds worth of guitar and microphone. What to do? Foreign country, young guys, not much language where to next? We hastily called for the club manager who called in Bob Xavier who in turn called the police. Not to put too fine a point on it but nobody seemed really bothered that our beautiful piece of Orville's best from good old Kalamazoo had gone missing, been nicked, filched, gone walkies.

We filled in forms, had many interviews, and tried our best to help the investigation but all to no avail. IT WAS GONE! This absolutely shattered us. The friendly Scottish band who were on with us kindly lent us what was required but the soul had been knocked out of the Crescents. We carried on as well as we could with our nightly gigs but something was definitely lacking. No sparkle was evident. We played well and efficiently but that was it. For about another two weeks we gigged and used the stage well but I think we all knew what was coming. There was no more effort to find the Gibson by any of the official departments and no offer of any sort of compensation from the club. I suppose one could see their point of view, but that didn't help our feeling of despondency and hurt. We talked at length and eventually formed a cunning plot (as Baldrick would say). We asked to be paid up to date in cash as we needed to buy another guitar, or so we told Bob

Xavier. This actually occurred and at about three o'clock the following morning we did what can only be described as a moonlight flit. We loaded all our gear under cover of darkness and drove off into the German night, fugitives from justice! We were about four hours from the Dutch border and hoped that our departure hadn't been noticed too early. Unfortunately it had. In the rear view mirror there appeared a huge American Chevrolet Impala in black and gold; Bob Xavier. Bob was an ex USA forces guy who had seen an opportunity and stayed on in Germany after his national service. He was Manfred Woitala's right hand man and as some would say, The Enforcer!

Bob motioned us to pull over and after some good old Crewe Anglo Saxon sign language we did so. He came to talk to us on the hard shoulder of the Autobahn and said that we should return and carry out our contract till the end of the month. Now we were reasonable guys and probably would have at least considered our options but Dave the bass man joined in. Dave was the youngest and quietest of the band and often just did as the other three of us suggested. To say we were amazed at Dave is an understatement. He looked Bob the Enforcer in the eye and gave him the most horrendous dressing down in the longest stream of four letter words I have ever heard in my life. No pause for breath, no letting up, just straight and to the point. He explained in graphic biological detail where Bob could insert his contract, his club, his car and as far as Dave was concerned the whole of West Germany! It was quite a sight to see Bob lost for words as he never had been ever before. Good on yer Dave, were the thoughts that came to the other three members of the band. The last words from a very irate Bob as he drove off were. 'You'll be stopped at the border, arrested and sent back.' Ulp-Ulp-Ulp.

Our intention as always was to cross the border into Holland on the road between Oldenburg in Germany and Groningen in the Netherlands. We arrived near the border and stopped about two hundred yards away to review the situation. There were many policeman, many dogs and lots of barbed wire. In fact it all looked quite like a scene from a war movie where the German Polizei were waiting to capture escapees from Colditz. A few more ulps were uttered and a plan thought up. This was quite a rural area with the main road running through lots of woods and fields in the local hinterland. We decided that for many years people would have traded and walked across the border from many small side roads and this would provide an opportunity for the great escape! We drove back a few hundred yards to a side road which we followed south for a mile or two, then turned west again to freedom and home!

All went well until we came to a customs post complete with a German Zollampt Grenzpolizei in his little hut. The barrier was raised and we sneaked up to the hut on foot to find the guard asleep! We tiptoed back to the van and push started it to avoid using the starter motor which was distinctly noisy, and as we neared the barrier I put my foot down and we made a mad dash across. Freedom at last. Hooray – hooray! We celebrated after a few yards by getting out of the van and singing Rule Britannia and having a wee, but not at the same time. Daft really but we were on an extreme high having been threatened with arrest and more in a foreign country. Little did I then know but the next time I was to return to Germany was with the Ministry of Defence as a NATO attached civilian.

I am not sure how my exploits in North Western Germany in 1965 would have been successfully explained if anyone had known about them in 1979.

We eventually arrived back in England after getting stranded in a minefield on the Belgian coast by taking the wrong turn, trying still to avoid main roads. We successfully negotiated reversing through red signs with skulls and explosive signs on them till after about ten minutes we were on safe ground. Scary or what? This was only twenty years after the war ended and the whole of the Franco-Belgian coasts were full of old military equipment and mines which had been neglected. England at last – home – safe, but as we were to learn, in the doghouse with Ken Smith and Darville Entertainments.

Ken was not amused that we had put in jeopardy his Anglo German contracts with all of his commission seemingly going up in smoke. We put our side of the story and came to a reasonably amicable truce agreeing that we would carry on with him after a short break cum holiday to clear the air. After about a week of kicking our heels we were off again gigging all over the UK as normal and trying to earn a living as well as we could. Eventually the time came to get off down to Abbey Road to record our third disc. The day came and we met up with Bob Barratt down at the studio and set about enthralling the world of vinyl and groove.

Bernard and Dave had written a song in Germany that we liked and persuaded Bob to make it our next A side. It was called, 'It Could Well Be' and was definitely in the Tom Jones style of 'It's not Unusual'. Dave played a heavy keyboard riff with Bernard following along with a suitable guitar part to try for as big a sound as we could with only three players as I was strictly vocals only. For all of our releases I was contracted as the singer Phil Ryan, with the others being paid as session musicians. Bob explained to us that using this method we would get more money even if we had a hit. I would get the royalties for sales which would be supplemented by three session fees. Of course all the money went into the band fund for equal shares at the end of each week, so instead of sharing just the royalties four ways we had the session money as well. I can't remember how much we are talking about but not a lot. I seem to remember that total royalties for Mary Don't You Weep were about £75 and session fees were about £9 per man per session of three hours. Now you might think that was ridiculously low but you have to remember that the average weekly wage in 1964 was about £12 to £15. So, in fact, our total for Mary was worth about seven weeks wages, which when you think about it was well worth all our efforts. But more to the point was the absolutely fantastic experience of recording at Abbey Road, doing Radio Luxembourg and meeting lots of great people. I can well remember sitting outside Norrie Paramours office with Dennis King and Patsy Anne Noble who were two of his artists. 'Norrie won't be long,' his secretary had said when who should walk out of the door but Cliff Richard and Bruce Welch who were also part of Norrie's stable.

However the sad part of this episode was that the EMI hierarchy decided that our latest effort was not commercial enough to justify a release and that they were ending our deal as per clause, whatever it might be, of our contract. We were quite stunned by this and very disappointed but business is business and that was that. They were quite within their rights to cancel with no compensation but it made us realise what a cut-throat game we were in and we spent many hours licking our wounds as they say. But life must go on and go on it did. We still had many good friends in parts of the UK who were always pleased to book The Crescents and see us in their club or dance hall. We were still travelling long ways to get to gigs with many a weekend being Scotland for Friday and Saturday nights and then down to Sheffield for a Sunday lunchtime session. We were still working well and being paid reasonable money for our labours. But something was missing from the old days. It was difficult to put it into words but our performance became very routine with not a lot of get up and go involved. We had taken a good few knocks what with the German fiasco and the EMI experience. Also at that time our contract with Ken Smith was to involve an increase in commission to Ken, with him going up to 25% of our gross take instead of the 20% we were paying for our first two years. We were all adamant that this could not happen, contract or no contract, and we put this to him. He wasn't best pleased but I think he could see that it was either this, or no more Phil Ryan and The Crescents.

We had some nice gigs as sort of short residences such as Neptune's Moorings in Preston Brook near Runcorn, The Belfry (well before golf), The Stormont Hall in Gretna Green and quite a few good regular venues. But things became very mundane and even at times boring. Now when you are doing a job you love, with a guitar, a van and an audience and things get boring it is time to take a long hard look at the world of music.

Chapter Eighteen

The End is Nigh

The headline says it all.

Group "sick and tired of travelling"

AFTER a career in the the world of "pop" music which has lasted three years, during which time they have made three records and given perform- ances in all parts of this country and even as far afield as the Continent, Phil Ryan and The Crescents, Crewe's only remaining big- time professional b e a t group, is to disband.

I was given the news in a tele- phone conversation with the group's Thornton Hough (Wirral) based manager, Mr Ken Smith, of Darville Entertainments, who told me that the group would officially break up early this month (May).

Why has the decision to bow out been taken? Ken told me that the boys were absolutely sick and tired of the endless travelling which they have to do to keep up their appearances at

Birkenhead (bass and organist) plans to stay in the "pop" industry and is joining "The Times"—a Runcorn group, and Bernard Hibbert (lead guitar) intends to start a new career in the credit clothing business.

The remaining member of the Crescents is Roger Keay (drum- mer) who, at the time of writing, was not quite sure what he would do when the group breaks up.

I understand that a final fare- well dance to Phil and the Crescents is to be arranged at the Civic Hall in Nantwich very shortly. Everyone who attends the dance will be presented with a souvenir photograph of the group.

Incidentally, other attractions at the Civic Hall in the near future include The Four Pennies and Unit Four plus Two.

✻ ✻ ✻

"Sounds 86"—this is the title of a beat contest open to groups from all parts of Cheshire and the North Midlands which is being organised to take place at the Civic Hall, Nantwich, in about a month's time.

We were all quietly thinking the same thing but nobody actually mentioned the F word, Finishing, until one day that is, when Roger out of the blue said, 'I'm fed up with all of this.' We all looked at him then looked at each other and realised that the end of the road was near. This was early in 1966 almost four years after I had joined forces with Bernard and the early band. In fact as I write this I become quite sad and nostalgic that what we had all achieved by our hard work and comradeship was about to end. What to do was the question.

We all had different ideas for our individual futures. We informed Ken that we had all reached a decision and as of May 1st 1966 Phil Ryan and the Crescents would cease to exist. In fact Ken agreed that the band had run its course and the best idea was to end it all before it became a drag and an imposition. At this time we had lots of chat and discussion as to what we would all do with our lives after the rigours of being on the road for four years. It ended up with all of us not having a clue at the time but we were all optimistic and thought undoubtedly, like Mr Micawber, that something would turn up!

Ken Smith rang me one day and said he had been on the phone to one of his contacts, a guy called Reg Calvert. Now we had played for Reg at quite a lot of his gigs throughout the Midlands and I realised that anything that involved Reg would be of interest. Ken told me that Glen Dale was leaving the Fortunes and he had talked to Reg about me being a possible replacement for Glen. Was I interested? Was I indeed? The Fortunes were a fantastic group who were good players, good singers and nice guys as well. They had recorded quite a few hits and at that time were the biggest name on the group circuit for South Yorkshire clubs, earning very good money for top gigs. People in the business would often look down their noses at the mention of northern clubs, but the reality was that they were well organised, well supported, and paid great money. At Dialhouse WMC near Sheffield Wednesday's ground we had a revolving stage, full stage lighting batons, proper tabs and follow-spots at the back.

I got straight back to Ken who organised a sort of meet and audition with The Fortunes and off I went to the Cosmo Ballroom in Carlisle which was about one hundred and fifty miles away from Crewe and was where they were gigging that night. I arrived and eventually found the band in the back dressing room sorting out their set for the night. I introduced myself and was also introduced to the members of the group. I can vividly remember sitting on the dressing room table singing Roy Orbison's 'In Dreams' with one of the Fortunes playing his guitar as my backing. Why I chose that song I will never know, but at least I got through it reasonably well and kept my fingers crossed for the next few days hoping to hear that soon I would become a Fortune.

At that time Reg Calvert was very much into all aspects of the group business. He was a manager, an agent, a promoter as well as general adviser and factotum to many, many well know bands. His best band by a mile was Screaming Lord Sutch and the Savages, a completely different kettle of fish to the Fortunes, who were probably more popular owing to chart successes with 'Here it Comes Again' and 'You've Got Your Troubles'. We gigged with The Savages many times and were always absolutely stunned by their drive and stage presence. With fantastic players like Carlo Little, Paul Nicholas, Richie Blackmore and others they couldn't go wrong in our eyes and whenever we gigged with them we knew we were in for a treat with the best Rock and Blues music ever heard from a British band.

After my Carlisle trip and audition I sat and waited for a few days and then the whole thing collapsed in the worst way imaginable. Reg, as one of his initiatives, part owned a pirate radio station called Radio London or Radio City, based somewhere on a ship or an old fort in the Thames estuary. Things did not go well with the co-owner and Reg went to have a clear the air meeting with Oliver Smedley at his home in Saffron Walden. To this day things have never ever been made clear but Reg and Oliver Smedley must have argued and off went Oliver to return with a shotgun, primed and loaded. The eventual outcome was that things must have become heated and a struggle ensued which finished up with Reg being shot dead on Smedley's doorstep. The whole of the pop world was stunned by this event and nobody really knew what to do with the Calvert promotions, the bands, or the rest of the business. Unfortunately for me this was the end of the Phil Ryan into the Fortunes saga, but my misfortune was nothing compared to the Calvert family loss.

We were still gigging along and wondering where the world would take us and where we all would be in three months' time. As the agreed finishing time got nearer and nearer Dave announced that he was going to take up an offer to join The Times, a Birmingham band which we had had lots of contact with over the previous months. So, Dave was off to join The

Times and eventually Roger went the same way to the same band, which became a sort of half Times and half Crescents. A bit later Bernard decided to keep on the pro circuit and join forces with a girl singer from Crewe called Val Hayes. He and Val had played and sung in bands together before the formation of the Crescents, so they rapidly progressed and formed The Avocado Pair and won Opportunity Knocks for three weeks on the trot. As for Dave and Roger, the Times worked well for some months along with Jim Simpson who became manager to Ozzie Osbourne and Black Sabbath. Both became better musicians playing regularly and eventually both joined Hedgehopper's Anonymous who had charted in previous years. After that they both moved on to become part of Sandy Shaw's backing group. Dave stayed with Sandy for quite a few years and travelled the world with her playing far flung outposts of the music business and making the most of his keyboard talents.

That left yours truly! Little old me. What could I do, what should I do, what ought I to do? I had thought earlier on in life, before the failed A levels, of becoming a PE teacher or Drama teacher. I had five reasonable O levels including the necessary English and Maths, and at that time the Minister for Education, Tony Crosland, announced that Britain needed ten thousand more teachers. Colleges and universities lowered their admittance levels to allow for this and five O levels became the entry requirement. To cut a long story short I had an interview and was accepted to become a first year student in the September of that year. I must add here that I was accepted for entry only after I agreed to the request from the Head of PE to have my hair cut!

On the musical front the Scorpions, a local Crewe band had heard that I was leaving the Crescents and stepped in. They were managed by Ron Ellwood, whose wife was my mother's cousin and son Jonty played in the band. We had a few meetings and I was in, alongside my old Hot Rod Drummer Dave Heaps. We formed a good group and within weeks we were playing many gigs, quite a lot for Ken Smith and Darville Entertainments. But as they say, that is a story for another day and possibly another book!

As I come to the end of this walk through my memories a few questions arise. Did I enjoy it? Absolutely! Did I learn a lot? A fantastic lot! Would I have changed anything? Not much, except to try for a better recording experience. I met some great people, saw some great bands, gigged with the best and the most famous. As a young lad from Crewe I shared the next peg in the dressing room to Bill Haley, chatted to Ben E King and gigged alongside the immortal Beatles. It can't get much better than that. I feel immensely privileged to have been able to do what any other young guy of my era would have given their right arm for. I have great memories that will never disappear, and still meet and chat with friends and band members from those far off distant days. All in all a great time with *A BAND ON THE ROAD!*

But wait a minute!   What of the future?

Well what d'y'know. The next step is here. Watch this space!

The Scorpions 1966